PERFECT SOFTWARE

and other illusions about testing

Also Available from Dorset House Publishing

Adrenaline Junkies and Template Zombies: Understanding Patterns of Project Behavior
by Tom DeMarco, Peter Hruschka, Tim Lister, Steve McMenamin,
Suzanne Robertson, and James Robertson
ISBN: 978-0-932633-67-5   Copyright ©2008   248 pages, softcover

Best Practices for the Formal Software Testing Process: A Menu of Testing Tasks
by Rodger D. Drabick   foreword by William E. Perry
ISBN: 978-0-932633-58-3   Copyright © 2004   312 pages, softcover

An Introduction to General Systems Thinking: Silver Anniversary Edition
by Gerald M. Weinberg
ISBN: 978-0-932633-49-1   Copyright © 2001   304 pages, softcover

iTeam: Putting the "I" Back into Team
by William E. Perry
ISBN: 978-0-932633-68-2   Copyright © 2008   est. 208 pages   softcover

Peopleware: Productive Projects and Teams, 2nd ed.
by Tom DeMarco and Timothy Lister
ISBN: 978-0-932633-43-9   Copyright ©1999   264 pages, softcover

Surviving the Top Ten Challenges of Software Testing: A People-Oriented Approach
by William E. Perry and Randall W. Rice
ISBN: 978-0-932633-38-5   Copyright © 1997   216 pages, softcover

**System Testing with an Attitude: An Approach That Nurtures
Front-Loaded Software Quality**
by Nathan Petschenik   ISBN: 978-0-932633-46-0   Copyright © 2005   368 pages, softcover

**Working Up to Project Management: How Crushing Rocks at the Asphalt Plant
Prepared Me for Government Work**
by Dwayne Phillips
ISBN: 978-0-932633-66-8   Copyright ©2008   216 pages, softcover

---

For More Information

✔ Contact us for prices, shipping options, availability, and more.

✔ Visit Dorsethouse.com for savings, reviews, downloads, and more.

DORSET HOUSE PUBLISHING
*An Independent Publisher of Books on
Systems and Software Development and Management. Since 1984.*
3143 Broadway, Suite 2B   New York, NY 10027   USA
1-800-DH-BOOKS   1-800-342-6657
212-620-4053   fax: 212-727-1044
info@dorsethouse.com   www.dorsethouse.com

PERFECT SOFTWARE

and other illusions about testing

Gerald M. Weinberg

DORSET HOUSE PUBLISHING
3143 BROADWAY, SUITE 2B
NEW YORK, NEW YORK 10027

Library of Congress Cataloging-in-Publication Data

Weinberg, Gerald M.
  Perfect software--and other illusions about testing / Gerald M. Weinberg.
    p. cm.
  Includes bibliographical references and index.
  ISBN 978-0-932633-69-9 (alk. paper)
  1. Computer software--Testing. 2. Computer software--Quality control.
  3. Computer software--Reliability. I. Title.
  QA76.76.T48W395 2008
  005.1'4--dc22

                        2008027598

Quantity discounts are available from the publisher. Call (800) 342-6657 or (212) 620-4053 or e-mail info@dorsethouse.com. Contact same for examination copy requirements and permissions. To photocopy passages for academic use, obtain permission from the Copyright Clearance Center: (978) 750-8400 or www.copyright.com.

Trademark credits: All trade and product names are either trademarks, registered trademarks, or service marks of their respective companies, and are the property of their respective holders and should be treated as such.

Cover design by David McClintock
Front cover image by Bart Sadowski, ©iStockphoto.com/Blueberries
Author photograph by Steven M. Smith, stevenmsmith.com

Distributed in the UK and EEC by Computer Bookshops Ltd., based in Birmingham, England (computerbookshops.com); in the English language in Singapore, the Philippines, and Southeast Asia by Alkem Company (S) Pte. Ltd., Singapore; and in the English language in India, Bangladesh, Sri Lanka, Nepal, and Mauritius by Prism Books Pvt., Ltd., Bangalore, India.

Printed in the United States of America

Library of Congress Catalog Number: 2008027598

ISBN: 978-0-932633-69-9

                             12 11 10 9 8 7 6 5 4 3

Acknowledgments

A book is a product, a software product, in a way. Like any viable software product, a book should be tested prior to release to the public to minimize the risk of its not being useful to its readers. To my team of book testers—James Bach, Michael Bolton, Fiona Charles, Elisabeth Hendrickson, Pradeep Soundararajan, and Dani Weinberg, who together detected dozens of bugs in early drafts of this manuscript—I give wholehearted thanks. I made the bugs originally and it was my job to eliminate or fix them, so if any remain, it's my responsibility, not theirs.

To my clients and students from all over the world, I give thanks for their having contributed the stories and examples that add flesh to the bones on which this book is built. All the examples are authentic and all the stories are true, though most have been disguised in some way to protect confidentiality.

Should you, my readers, find some bug that I missed or some story or example that fits, I hope you will bring it to my attention. I thank you in advance for joining the test team.

Contents

Preface

More than half a century ago, when I started in the computer business, computers were extremely rare and precious. I was barely more than a teenager when I found myself sitting at a console in front of a huge room full of hardware that comprised perhaps 10 percent of the computing power in the world. I could turn it off with a press of my finger—and sometimes did.

If you were willing to wait your turn, you could rent all that power for an hour for approximately twice my monthly salary. Today, computers are so affordable that I have actually given away machines that are 50,000 times faster than those early models, with 50,000 times the memory. These giveaway machines, which are so compact and lightweight that I easily can carry one in my briefcase, don't account for even a billionth of the computing power in the world today.

Yes, I've seen technology come a long way, but it crept up on me gradually. I didn't really take note of the changes until a few years ago when I heard a newscast reporting on the scrubbing of a rocket launch at Cape Canaveral. As the announcers wrapped up their report, one commented, "NASA says it was a computer software error."

The second announcer replied, "Isn't it strange that something so simple and common as a computer could make such a mistake?"

"Yes," responded the first. "Wouldn't you think they would test their software?"

* * *

Yes, I think they would test their software. In fact, I'm sure they did. Evidently, though, the announcer thought testing must inevitably lead to a perfect product.

I couldn't stop thinking about this dialogue and the broadcaster's unrealistic expectations. At first, I simply shrugged and told myself, "Such is the ignorance of the general public about software testing," but it was too late to shrug it off. My consciousness was now raised. I began to see how even the managers at my software-building clients display the same ignorance. *Especially* the managers. Software testing was driving them crazy.

I'm an empathic person, and when people around me suffer, I suffer with them. I could see that the software managers were suffering, along with their employees and customers. I could also now see that almost all of them were suffering not so much because testing was complicated or time-consuming or laborious; they were suffering because of their unreasonable expectations and fallacious models about software testing.

Finally, I decided to do what I always seem to do when I find ignorance causing pain: I wrote about the problem and probable solutions. What I wrote eventually became this book.

* * *

When I wrote *The Psychology of Computer Programming* many years ago, I intended it to help people who want to understand programming. [1] Quite a few people have told me it helped, so perhaps, in part, the success of that book inspired me to write this book: to help people who want to understand testing.

My intended audience is broad: I envision this book in the hands of professional testers, developers, consumers, analysts, designers, programmers, all of their managers, and all of their coworkers.

Most *professional testers* will know most of what's in this book, but I hope that by reading on, they will see new ways to communicate what they know—to *their* managers, developers, coworkers, and customers.

I'd like to help both *developers* and *testers* understand what their *managers* face when they confront software testing issues.

I'd like to help *customers*—the people who buy the software—to be better-informed consumers.

And, since everyone is affected by software today—and hurt by poorly tested software—I'd like to help *everyone* to care more about testing.

Because I hope to reach a broad audience, I've chosen to use plain language wherever possible, avoiding highly technical terms and overly detailed analyses. (For those who are interested in learning more technical detail about software testing, I point to some particularly solid books in the Additional Reading section at the end of this book.) To keep my focus on helping people who want to understand testing, I've organized the book around the questions that puzzle the most people:

Why do we have to bother testing when it just seems to slow us down?

Why can't people just build software right in the first place, so it doesn't need testing?

Do we have to test everything?

Why not just test everything?

What is it that makes testing so hard?

Why does testing take so long?

Is perfect software even possible?

Why can't we just accept a few bugs?

April 2008
Albuquerque, New Mexico   G.M.W.

PERFECT SOFTWARE

and other illusions about testing

1

Why Do We Bother Testing?

". . . the realization came over me with full force that a good part of the remainder of my life was going to be spent in finding errors in my own programs."

—William Aspray and Martin Campbell-Kelly, *Computer: A History of the Information Machine* (New York: Westview Press, 2004), p. 167.

Suppose you have a great idea for a software program that will compute the ideal investment strategy. You plan to use the software to turn your meager life savings into millions. You write the software, and you're sure you've done it perfectly. Now what would you do?

Would you test the program before investing every penny you've saved based on its investment-strategy advice?

Would you test it if someone else had written the program?

If you answered the first question, "No, I wouldn't bother to test it," don't read any further. This book is not for people who think that they can write a perfect program and be perfectly sure that it is perfect. If you also answered no to the second question, you must believe that human thinking can be perfect. Answering no to either or both of these questions means, to me, that you are in a category of people who will not enjoy this book because you won't understand why it's necessary. Put it down right now. Spare yourself further pain.

Humans are not perfect thinkers.

If your thinking were perfect, you would not need testing. If you believe that you must always be perfect, then you would find the existence of testing or testers rather upsetting, because it would imply that your thinking cannot be perfect. But if you say, "Well, before I invested my life savings, I might want to do a little testing," then you won't always be upset by the very idea of testing. You should read on.

If you're still reading, welcome. You're showing me both that you are a real human being and that you know that you are. Real human beings know that no matter how hard they try to do a perfect job, they will sometimes make mistakes. Real human beings also know they are not alone in their fallibility, and that other human beings are similar. Knowing this, you just might enjoy reading this book, because it's about how real humans can make decisions that are better than they could make without testing. Better decisions, in fact, than those made by people who think they must always be perfect. But only better, not perfect.

We need to make decisions about software.

At the simplest level, people are doing testing all the time. We often run and analyze tests without even knowing it. Here, in my own words from my journal, are some tests I did while writing this book, tests I really didn't think of, consciously, as tests.

* * *

Journal entry 1:

"I want a Web-writing application compatible with Mac OS X. A review I read described a rather wonderful application, full of features that I'd like to have. Then I read that it doesn't run under OS X.

"**End of test:** The application doesn't meet my constraint (system compatibility). I will not buy it."

> Recap: We test to be sure our software isn't rejected
> because it fails to satisfy an essential customer

4

constraint. (Note: This *is* a test, even though I never touched a keyboard. More on that later.)

Journal entry 2:

"I'm still looking for a Web-writing application, and today I ran across a five-star review of a freeware photo-cataloging program. I was about to download it when I realized that the photo-cataloging program won't do the work of a Web-writing application. I don't have more than ten photos that I want to keep, so no matter how wonderful it is, who needs a photo-cataloging program to manage ten pictures?

"**End of test:** The application doesn't meet any requirement (I'm looking for a Web-writing application), so I don't need it."

> Recap: We test to be sure our software isn't rejected because it doesn't do the things people want it to do. (Note, once again, that this was a test I did without banging any keys.)

Journal entry 3:

"I've found a free Web-writing application that runs under OS X and does the things I want it to do. The promotional material indicates that it can be downloaded and used for one month for free, with the option of enabling it permanently with a key that I can buy for $49. I've downloaded the trial copy and tried to install it, but the installation failed because I don't have the right model internal disk drive.

"**End of test:** I cannot install the application on my configuration without voiding my warranty, so I won't buy it. My search continues."

> Recap: We test to be sure our software isn't rejected because it imposes unacceptable costs and/or requirements on our customers. (Note: I finally touched a key, but only one, to perform this test.)

Journal entry 4:

"I found another Web-writing application that runs under OS X and offers a free 30-day trial. I've downloaded it and installed it successfully. So that is good, but when I opened a Web page that I had under construction and made a small modification, the application crashed when I tried to save the page.

"**End of test:** If a function this common fails, I cannot have much confidence in the application, so I won't buy this one either."

> Recap: We test to be sure our software isn't rejected because its failures destroy customer confidence.

Journal entry 5:

"I've finally discovered a Web-writing program that runs on the Web itself, meets all of my constraints, doesn't crash on the first few things I try to do, and permits me to save my work. All that is great, but there is a *major* drawback: Each save takes more than a minute.

"**End of test:** I cannot afford to wait more than a minute each time I save my work. Such performance would cost me at least a half-hour during my workday. I can't use the program."

> Recap: We test to be sure our software isn't rejected because it forces our customers to waste their time.

Journal entry 6:

"A friend recommended a Web-writing application she uses. It runs on OS X and, according to her, never crashes. It has the features I want—and costs $999.

"**End of test:** I don't want a Web-writing application badly enough to justify spending almost a thousand dollars, so I won't buy it."

> Recap: We test to be sure our software isn't rejected because it's too costly for most of our customers.

* * *

So, after all of these tests, what did I end up doing? I kept on using my old, reliable, orphan, unsupported software, under my old operating system, OS 9. I decided that, at least until further tests of other software would guide me to change my decision, the old way would work well enough.

What I've described above could be called "acceptance testing," but when you turn it around, you see the reasons—the reasons for testing from the producer's point of view. You test to see whether your software product will *sell*. And "selling" includes cases in which you think users will be "forced" to use the software, such as when they are employees of an organization that mandates its use. Don't kid yourself. Software users will find ways of not using software that they don't want to use. So, even internal users have to be "sold"—though not all testers think of their work this way.

Decisions can be risky.

Obviously, we can make decisions without testing at all. Choosing a lottery number is a decision that can't be helped much by our having additional information (such as test-sample results). If it could, it wouldn't be a lottery. But in many decisions, having some additional information *can* improve our chances of a satisfactory outcome. Expressed another way, information can help reduce risk.

If the decisions concern software that is being built, borrowed, or bought, testing may be one of the ways to obtain that risk-reducing information. Good testing involves balancing the need to mitigate risk against the risk of trying to gather too much information. Before you even begin to test, ask yourself: *What questions do I have about this product's risks? Will testing help answer these questions?*

If you don't have questions about a product's risks, then there's no reason to test. If you have at least one such question, then ask: *Will these tests cost more to execute than their answers will be worth?*

Let's see how this works: About the time I was executing the last of my Web-writing-applications tests, one of my clients asked my advice about a series of tests for the software in an embedded

7

heart-monitor pacemaker. It may seem obvious that the risks associated with variations in performance in an embedded heart-monitor pacemaker are vastly different from the risks associated with variations in performance in Web-writing applications, so do you think I recommended the same testing process I used for finding a personal Web-writing application? Do you imagine I recommended that my client install random freeware pacemakers into live patients until he found something he liked? Why not?

You know that the decision about which pacemaker software to use has rather different consequences than the decision about which personal Website editor to use. But that's a rather extreme and obvious contrast. In general, though the answers to questions posed by testing should have the potential of reducing risk, assessment of risk is subjective. It has to be, because it's about the future, and—as Woody Allen, Niels Bohr, and Yogi Berra all reportedly have quipped—we can predict anything except the future.

Risk is also subjective because the same risk feels different to different people. Some folks wouldn't hesitate to jump out of an airplane, yet fear a hypodermic needle so much that they won't get a flu shot. Others won't jump out of a plane under any circumstances, but they don't think twice about getting a flu shot every year.

The following exchange illustrates how a person's ideas about risk influence that person's ideas about what is proper testing. Denise, a development manager, has been having trouble getting Ralph, a developer, to do effective unit testing before turning his work over to the professional testers.

> Denise: "Do you think you're doing an adequate job of unit testing?"
> Ralph: "Yes, I'm very thorough."
> Denise: "So your present project is ready to pass to the testing people?"
> Ralph: "Absolutely."
> Denise: "Okay, since you're so sure it's adequately tested, I'm going to make you the following generous offer: If fewer than three bugs turn up in your component during testing, I will give you a raise.

> But if three or more bugs turn up during testing, you won't earn a raise this year."
> Ralph: "Um . . ."
> Denise: "Um what?"
> Ralph: "Could I just have the component back for a few little tests I want to do?"

In this exchange, Denise raises the consequences of errors slipping through unit testing, and Ralph's idea of what constitutes an adequate unit test suddenly changes.

Testing can provide information that reduces risk.

Different people, different projects, different times, may mean different perceptions of risks and thus different sorts of questions that testing might be designed to help answer. For example, one basic question we might ask is,

> *Does the software do what we want it to do?*

Anything not worth doing is not worth doing right, so if the answer to this question is no, then we don't need to ask other questions. Suppose however, that despite the software's considerable shortcomings, we want more information, asking,

> *If the software doesn't do what we want it to do, how much work will be involved in fixing it?*

Testing cannot answer this question by itself, but it can supply information that, combined with information about our development process, helps us identify work to be done and reduce the risks in estimating what it will take to do that work.

> *Does the software not do what we don't want it to do?*

In some ways, this is the question most easily associated with risk. Some of the unwanted things software might do could cause damage to life, limb, or property. More than one organization has been killed by software that did something it didn't want it to do. Sadly, more than one person has been killed, too.

9

Does the software do what we intended?

This question is about doing right those things that are worth doing. If something is worth doing, it's worth doing right. Answering this question reduces the risk that the software is not doing what was intended.

Will the software do what our customers want?

Anyone selling a product knows the fear that customers simply will not buy, or will buy and be unsatisfied. Testing cannot predict how many people will buy your product, but it can help reduce the risk that people won't buy it because it doesn't do what they're willing to pay for.

Will the software satisfy other business needs?

If customers won't buy your products, your business won't succeed. But even if they do buy, you could lose money on each sale if, for instance, the technical support cost exceeds the price of the product. Testing can help reduce the risk of unanticipated repair costs and support.

What are the likelihood and consequences of failure?

Since testing provides information that can reduce risk of failure, the amount of testing we do is influenced by both the likelihood and consequences of failure, as suggested by the following table:

		Likelihood of Failure	
		Lower	**Higher**
Consequences of Failure	**Lower**	least testing	moderate testing
	Higher	moderate testing	most testing

Summary

Testing has its roots in psychology, in the study of the behavior of the human brain. If humans were perfect thinkers, we wouldn't need to test our work. If we were unemotional robots, we would always use testing in a rational way, to reduce risk in our decisions. If we were identical clones, we would all assess risks in the same way. But we are imperfect, irrational, value-driven, diverse human beings. Therefore, we test, and we test our testing.

Common Mistakes

1. *Striving for perfection:* We'll see in Chapter 3 that perfection is impossible to achieve. Trying to do the impossible will kill you.

2. *Not making decisions:* A manager's job is to make management decisions. Don't ask testers questions like, "Is the software ready to ship?" That's the manager's decision. The testers' job is to provide information (but not all the information) that informs that decision.

3. *Not recognizing all the information needed for decision-making:* By not taking *all* relevant information into consideration when making a decision, you're risking management, staff, and customer satisfaction. For example, if you fail to consider your customers' special needs and merely listen to the opinions of developers and testers, you're not likely to have happy customers—regardless of what your technical staff thinks is "right."

4. *Putting wrong priorities on various risks:* If you're afraid of losing your promotion if you don't ship a product on schedule, you may ship a buggy product that costs your organization millions. Of course, if all you care about is your promotion, then as long as you no longer have responsibility for the product, you won't care when the cost of quick shipping comes due.

5. *Believing testing can improve a product:* Testing gathers information about a product; it does not fix things it finds that are wrong. Testing does not improve a product; the improving is done by people fixing the bugs that testing has uncovered. Often when managers say, "Testing takes too long," what they should be saying is, "Fixing the bugs in the product takes too long"—a different cost

category. Make sure you're accounting for effort and time under the correct cost category.

6. *Believing there's a "testing phase" during which all testing—and only testing—is done:* Software testing expert and author James Bach likes to ask his clients whether they have a testing phase in their process. James reports, "Almost everyone says yes. Then I suggest that the 'testing phase' is really the 'fixing phase.' How do I know? Because the testing phase seems so often to end before testing is completed, yet it is much rarer to see a product ship before the people who make that decision believe that every really important problem has been fixed."

James then asks his clients to consider driving a car: "When is the 'look out the windshield phase' of driving? Pretty much all driving is looking out the windshield! It's not a phase. Saying 'testing takes too long' is a bit like saying 'safe driving takes too long.'"

And, of course, safe driving often takes longer—if you don't consider what happens when you have an accident because you're not looking out the windows.

2

What Testing Cannot Do

"Have no fear of perfection—you'll never reach it."
—Salvador Dali, Spanish Surrealistic Painter (1904–1989)

Imagine you are an executive in charge of a multimillion-dollar logistics system. The company president, Benito, is a dynamic, forceful character known for firing people in staff meetings when they don't give him the answers he wants. He is eager to have the system rolled out. He's putting pressure on you. You go to the project manager, who reports to you, and ask,

"How's progress on the system?"

The project manager replies, "I don't know."

What would you do now? Quite likely, you'd want more information than "I don't know." There are various ways to acquire it:

a. Maybe torture will work.

Pull out the project manager's fingernails one at a time until she squeals, "Oh, yes, I do know. It's great!" If necessary, proceed to toenails.

b. Maybe promoting a toady will work.

Fire the project manager and promote someone who says, "I do know." Repeat this step as needed.

c. Maybe gathering information will work.

Look for some information on what the program actually does when someone tries to use it in a realistic way.

If you want reliable information, *a* and *b* probably won't do the job, but *c* at least has a chance. Gathering information on what a program actually does when used is one form of what some people call "testing."

Information doesn't necessarily help reduce risk.

Managers in the software business frequently have to make risky decisions, which can be made less dangerous if based on answers to questions such as the following:

- *Do we ship now? Later? Ever?*
- *Do we cancel the project?*
- *Do we continue the project and add more resources?*
- *Do we reduce the scope of the project?*
- *Do we attempt to bring the product to a wider market?*
- *Do we sell this version of the product at a lower price?*

Of course, such decisions could be made in the complete absence of information—and they frequently are. More often, they're made after the decision-maker has obtained some bit of information, while resolutely ignoring other information that might be obtained. Since testing is an information-gathering process, there's always a question of whether it's worthwhile to pay for more testing. And that is another decision.

Someone in the organization has the authority to make decisions, with or without information. If that person will make the same decision no matter what additional information arises, there is little point in testing to gather more information. If Benito has decided to go forward with the new logistics system as is, why bother getting him more information? Why bother testing?

In fact, sometimes doing more testing adds to the risk. If Benito delays the product while waiting for more tests on the logistics system, he might enter the market too late. Or, he might go broke spending money on testing. So, we always have to consider money and time in the decision about whether to test: *Testing cannot be done in zero time and cannot be done for free.*

Sometimes, the information produced also adds to the risk. If the developers have information that something isn't working well, they may want to spend time fixing it. From the point of view of Benito, this could increase the risk of spoiling something that was working well enough to use.

You might think the real risk is in having a development organization you can't control, but here's another danger. If people sue you because of an error in software you developed and sold, they can subpoena the records of your development process. If the records indicate that your testers found this bug and you didn't fix it, you're in more trouble than if they'd never found it in the first place. Sometimes, ignorance really is (legal) bliss.

The same blissful-ignorance principle translates down to the individual manager, even if no lawsuit is involved. If there's a problem with the product in the field and the manager can honestly say, "I didn't know," the repercussions usually are less severe than if that manager knew but didn't do anything about it. The moral: Think carefully about what may qualify as too much information. But think even more carefully about which of your goals are foremost. Are you trying to produce a successful product, or avoid lawsuits, or simply advance your personal career?

We may not be using the information we're paying for.

There's never an easy answer to the question "Should we do more testing?" because information *can* guide risk reduction, but doesn't necessarily do so. Consequently, when I acceptance-tested a Web-writing application that didn't work well (see Chapter 1), it would have been easy for me to conclude, "This must not have been tested well!" Maybe, or maybe not. Perhaps it was well tested, but no one acted on the information. Testing is not fixing.

This observation leads to the question of whether you are *receiving* the information you're paying testers to produce. Sometimes, when testers don't generate reams of paper, it's easy to decide you're not getting your money's worth. You fall victim to equating information quality with data quantity (bug counts, pages of test reports, number of test cases run, and so on).

15

Be careful. This may be one of those situations in which an absence of information leads to the most important information. To obtain your money's worth from testing, you will have to continue the process of questioning and interpreting what's going on beyond what's stated explicitly in test reports.

Perhaps the testers are not uncovering vast quantities of bugs because they cannot install the software despite having spent six weeks of overtime in the attempt. If this is the case, the testers have uncovered critical information indeed. If they cannot install your application, what makes you think a user could do so?

Or, perhaps the testers do not understand the software. If they have only a vague idea of what it is expected to do, you may end up with little useful information about the software. You do, however, know something about information flow in the organization. If the testers have trouble understanding the software, perhaps one or two of the developers had similar trouble and wrote code that doesn't work.

Another possibility is that the testers don't know how to test, or aren't very good at it, or don't really care.

If you don't pursue the questions beneath the surface, you generally won't obtain your money's worth out of your investment in testing. Half of the complaints I hear about testing come from managers who fail to pursue *all* of the information in their test results. If you're not going to use the information generated, don't pay for tests.

Our decisions are emotional, not rational.

Because testing provides information that can help you take the risk out of decisions, you might think that everyone would love and value testing. But people have many psychological reasons for making decisions that have nothing to do with rational use of information. We've all heard the expression, "My mind is made up; don't confuse me with the facts." Some of us have even said it ourselves.

People have an emotional investment in not finding out that they've made mistakes. Some managers don't want to know that their project is headed down the slippery slope to failure. Some developers don't want people to know that their code is buggy.

Whenever you attempt to influence such emotion-laden factors, the interventions can easily backfire.

For example, suppose you establish a bonus scheme for developers who have low bug counts, hoping to motivate them to produce better code. This reward scheme can backfire because it calls even more attention to found bugs than may have been previously paid. This attention feeds into the developers' desire to have people not know about their bugs, which could lead different developers in different directions.

One developer might respond as you intended, and will view reward as an incentive to work more carefully and to test meticulously. For another, however, the same reward scheme could serve as an incentive to make the product difficult to test, the rationale being, "If they can't find it, it won't cost me my bonus."

Or, suppose you want to motivate your managers to ship products on time, so you conspicuously promote each manager whose product goes out the door on schedule. All goes as planned until the situation arises in which one of your managers has a project where the testers are reporting numerous problems. Because managers who have shipped products on time have been promoted, this manager thinks, *I want that promotion so I need to ship this on time, but those bug reports are getting in the way. I know what I'll do! I'll put the testers on another project until the developers have a chance to catch up.*

(Note to manager: In such situations, developers never catch up.)

Poor testing may be worse than no testing at all.

Poorly conceived tests or poorly executed tests—for purposes of this book, I lump these two categories into one, called "poor tests" or "bad tests"—may give you the impression that a product is better than it is, causing you to ship before it's ready. Or, poor tests may give you the impression that a product is worse than it actually is, causing you to defer shipping and lose potential benefits.

How can you recognize poor tests? There are numerous flavors of *not doing it well*, so many, in fact, that I cover poor tests and how to recognize them throughout this book. In the meantime, if you suspect that you're going to test poorly, consider not testing at all.

Your product may not be ready for testing.

At what point is your product ready for test? That question is not always easy to answer, but you can ask more-easily-answered questions to draw out information that will tell you when you're *not ready* for test:

- *Is there at least one question about your product that testing can help you answer?* If there's no question, then there's no reason to test.
- *Do you want to know the answer to that question?* If you don't want to know the answer, don't ask the question—that is, don't bother testing.
- *Are you merely idly curious about the results of testing?* If you're not going to evaluate or act on the answers to your questions, forget testing. It's too expensive to be used just to satisfy idle curiosity. Active curiosity, on the other hand, is an important attribute of effective testing, because you'll never know exactly what you should be looking for. So, if you are ready to spend some time exploring, being curious will help you get your money's worth out of testing—if you follow through on what you discover.
- *Can you agree with testers in advance as to what constitutes a* passed *test?* If you don't agree about what is a passed test and what isn't, what are you looking for from your tests?
- *Do you have agreement in advance on what a* successful *test would look like? An* unsuccessful *test?* Do you agree that any test that gives you new information is at least partially successful?
- *Do you think the outcome of testing will make your decisions for you?* Business decisions cannot be made from a purely technical perspective. Certainly use information from testing to color your business decisions, but don't substitute testing for business decisions. For example, it can be a good business decision to ship a system that fails one or more tests. Conversely, it can be a bad business decision to ship a system that passes all your tests.

Management has to consider other factors in addition to test results.
- *Conversely, is there any possible test outcome that would make you change your decisions?* If not, why would you want to know the outcome, let alone pay for it?

Summary

You don't have to test if, for any reason, you're not going to use the resulting information. And, if the information isn't going to be relevant or reliable, you'd better not use it, so don't bother to buy it in the first place.

Common Mistakes

1. *Not honoring testers:* If you aren't going to believe what the testers uncover, either you have the wrong people or you need to get serious about helping them build their credibility. Testing is never just a matter of hiring and hoping.

2. *Over-honoring testers:* If you let them make your decision for you, then you should step down and let them earn the manager's salary.

3. *Scapegoating testers:* Even worse than over-honoring testers is *pretending* to honor them—manipulating them to give you the answers you want, appearing to act on that "independent" assessment, then blaming them later if that assessment turns out to be damagingly wrong (or taking credit if it turns out to be right).

4. *Not using the information gleaned from testing or other sources:* If you're going to ignore information or go ahead with predetermined plans despite what the tests turn up, don't bother testing. (Actually, it can't really be considered information if you don't use it.)

5. *Making decisions that are emotional, not rational:* Not that you can be perfectly rational, but you can at least try to be calm and in control of your emotions when you make decisions.

6. *Not evaluating the quality of test data:* Numbers are just numbers. Learn to ask, "What was the process used to obtain this number?" "What does this number mean?" [2]

7. *Testing without adequate preparation:* By "adequate preparation," I mean that you must be prepared to recognize problems when they turn up, which may encompass as little as developing a basic understanding of the purpose and nature of the application under test. I don't mean that you will need to have identified a complete and unambiguous expected result for every test before you begin running that test. To be adequately prepared, you must also be *personally prepared:* prepared to learn, prepared to design, prepared to perform effectively.

8. *Failing to coordinate testing with the rest of a project:* If you're not going to give your developers needed time or resources to fix problems found in testing, testing will be a wasted effort, so just skip it. Testing is a technology-development-support activity that must be coordinated with the requirements, design, programming, documenting, manufacturing, and support processes. To coordinate testing with the rest of the project's cycles, consultant and testing expert James Bach asks himself three questions: *What can I do right now to be most of service on this project? What do I need to do now to get ready to be of service on the project tomorrow or next month? What test activity might need to be cut off now because we've reached 'good enough' and need those cycles for something new?*

9. *Rushing the testers:* Testing is often a subtle business. Pushing testers to test faster generally produces dangerously misleading results—especially when testers are frightened, tired, or cynical.

10. *Not insisting on due diligence from managers:* If you allow managers to plead ignorance of the test process as an excuse for allowing bugs to pass, you might as well not test. Beware of testers claiming "it's impossible to know if we've found all the bugs" to excuse what could truly be called negligence. Managers need to understand enough about testing to recognize the difference between negligence and an honest mistake. If they cannot, they need to develop test managers and leads whom they can trust to perform that evaluation for them.

11. *Assuming that others' decisions are not rational just because they don't agree with yours:* Many decisions that seem irrational are rational according to a different set of values. Remembering this principle can save an enormous amount of conflict among managers, testers, and developers.

12. *Not realizing there is more than one use for information from testing:* In many cases, project members might want to continue testing after delivering a product in order to collect information that will be useful to customer service and support staffs.

3

Why Not Just Test Everything?

"Testing may convincingly demonstrate the presence of bugs, but can never demonstrate their absence."

—Edsger W. Dijkstra, Computing Pioneer (1930–2002), "Programming as a discipline of mathematical nature," *Am. Math. Monthly*, 81 (1974), No. 6, pp. 608–12.

I was called in to consult recently by a test manager whose manager had demanded that he "test everything." It was not the first time I'd heard this impossible demand.

Why is it impossible? First of all, the human brain not only makes mistakes, its capacity is finite. Second, nobody lives forever. So, as much as we would like to perform all possible tests, we can't think of them, and, even if we could, we wouldn't live long enough to do them all. Besides, for most situations, it would cost too much—since the number of possible tests for any given program is infinite. Let's see why.

There are an infinite number of possible tests.

Let's think of the simplest program we could conceive of to test: a program whose function will be to respond to tapping on the space bar by putting a "Hello Dolly!" message on the screen. What would we test for? To keep it simple, we'd want to test that every time we pressed the space bar, we got the "Hello Dolly!" message, and every time we pressed any other key or combination of keys, we never got anything on the screen.

If you can't see inside the program, how many test cases would you need to execute in order to bet your life that you've tested all possibilities? Identify the number of test cases, write that number down, and then read the next paragraphs to see if you got it right.

Since you can't see inside the program, you have no idea what bizarre conditions the programmer might have set up. For example, the program might be designed so that everything looks normal on the outside unless the user types an extremely unlikely sequence of keystrokes. Suppose I set up the program so that if you hit, say, the W key, then the space bar three times, then the M key, then the space bar another three times, then the J key, then you type exactly 168 more keystrokes without once using the letter L, the program will put a message on the screen asking, "Whaaa?" Would your exhaustive set of test cases have detected this outlandish condition in which an unwanted and unexpected Whaaa response is hidden in the program?

Do you think these conditions are outlandish? Unrealistic? During a technical review of a supposedly highly secure application, we discovered that a programmer named Wanda Marilyn Jones (not her real name, but her real initials) had placed exactly this backdoor into the software, writing the password protection so that she could bypass the ordinary password protection, regardless of what the real password was set to be, thereby enabling her to break in at any time. A highly sophisticated test plan, executed under strict controls, had not found this backdoor, which lay hidden for three years until we performed a technical review. To paraphrase Edsger Dijkstra, "Testing can reveal the presence of bugs, not their absence."

Do you get the point by now? If you didn't guess that the number of tests required to exhaustively test software is infinite, or at least "a number greater than I could run in my lifetime," you didn't understand the point of this chapter. Now you do.

Notice that I didn't even mention the possibility of testing this program on different configurations, a problem commonly faced by product developers. If a program has to work on ten different CPUs, each with ten possible memory sizes and ten different disk-drive sizes, that would mean 10 times 10 times 10 different configurations that would have to be tested.

But that's way too simple for many real testing situations, where the tester has to deal with the added complexity inherent in having different manufacturers, drivers, operating system versions, other programs simultaneously operating, and combinations of other different peripheral devices, any of which could contain errors. Dealing "completely" with all possible configurations like this would necessitate quadrillions of different test cases. And that's not considering tests for all the different functions that program is supposed to perform with any of these configurations.

Even this immense number ignores sequence effects reflective of the order in which the tests are performed. If there are ten functions a user might invoke, it isn't enough to use ten different tests because they might produce different results if performed in different orders. So, instead of ten tests, we'd need ten factorial (10!) tests (over six million) to cover all sequences.

But that wouldn't be enough, either, because if the program has memory (and all real programs do), then the second time we perform a test sequence, it may not produce the same results as it did the first time.

And these immense numbers (all multiplied together) also ignore true randomness, like the exact nanosecond an external device causes an interrupt or the exact timing to the microsecond of when you strike, say, the J key. All in all, testing can be exhausting, but it can never be exhaustive.

Testing is, at best, sampling.

Since we can't test everything, any set of real tests is some kind of sample—a portion, piece, or segment that is in some way representative of a whole set of possible tests. We, of course, hope it's a *good* representative, but that brings up the question, "Good for whom?" Fundamentally, sampling is yet another psychological process—and an emotional one. A sample that satisfies one person may not satisfy another in the slightest.

So how do we decide what to sample? How do we know we're taking a large enough sample to adequately represent *everything*? How do we know we've taken an appropriate sample?

I was musing about this problem with my colleague Elisabeth Hendrickson as we watched my rain gauge during a rainstorm in Pecos Canyon, New Mexico. The gauge, which is attached to the exterior of my porch, had a small opening through which it was supposed to sample rain—which, at the time, consisted of large, widely spaced drops splattering on the ground every few seconds. It would have been an adequate rain gauge for Seattle, because it would have done well with a fine, misty rain that fell for hours, but when the Pecos storm stopped after ten minutes, the bottom of my gauge was completely dry, belying the fact that any rain had fallen.

But Elisabeth and I had seen the rain fall and, in fact, we were soaked. We quickly realized that the gauge was taking an inadequate sample when dealing with such huge drops falling several inches apart over the minutes the storm lasted. Elisabeth looked at my dripping beard and said, "*You* are a better rain gauge than the one on the porch."

Notice that it could have worked the other way. If just one or two of those huge drops had happened to fall into its small opening, the gauge might have reported a full quarter-inch of rain, which wasn't accurate either. We regularly see this same phenomenon in testing: We take a small sample—try a few things here and there—and end up under- or over-reporting the density of problems in the whole product.

The cost of information can exceed the cost of ignorance.

The impossibility of exhaustive testing squeezes us between two difficult and simultaneously desirable objectives:

1. We want to cover all interesting conditions.
2. We want to reduce the set of tests to a manageable, affordable level.

To understand what I mean by the first, consider the number of times testers stumble across a critical bug when they aren't looking for that particular type of bug. They find it because they are lucky (or unlucky, if they don't want to know about it), not because they were executing a set of meticulously designed tests intended to find that specific problem. The bug just appears, like an ant in your raisin bran. But is it pure luck? Is there some psychology to figuring out how to find more of these surprise bugs? I believe that part of the answer lies in expanding our idea of testing.

We can obtain more information with less testing—perhaps.

These days, many of the people I talk with are concerned with the second objective stated above—reducing the set of tests to a manageable, affordable level. They're asked, or commanded, to subsist and even thrive with smaller teams and greater responsibilities.

In one of the more extreme cases described to me, a tester sought a consultant's advice on handling the following dilemma: "We were just downsized from a team of thirty testers to three, but we're still supposed to 'ensure' the product. How do I decide what to test?"

One argument would say that testers can't "ensure" anything at all so they shouldn't even try. But that argument won't persuade an executive staff struggling to keep a firm afloat during rough economic times. So what to do? Admittedly, a downsized team can't do everything the larger staff used to do, but it can pick and choose from among the tests it could possibly perform. It can identify the tests that make the best use of limited resources.

The consultant's advice was grounding: "First of all, recognize that any set of tests is a sampling strategy and then, no matter how many or how few your resources, choose the best representative set of tests you can."

Imagine you are about to dine at the Testing Buffet.

You stand at the head of a long table full of use cases, boundary conditions, compatibility tests, interaction tests, permissions matrices, and so on, holding a single plate. The Testing Buffet allows a diner only a couple of trips through the line, so you know that you'd better choose wisely. What should you do?

Well, if you have ever watched people faced with this situation in a food buffet, you know that different personalities attack problems in different ways. Some people will complain to the maître d' or waiter about the size of the plates and continue whining throughout the meal, spoiling everybody else's meal. Others will simply turn around and walk away in a huff because they believe they shouldn't be limited in the amount they may eat.

Some people will start at the head of the line and fill the plate with the first two dishes that appeal to them. Is this wise? Maybe at a restaurant, but probably not when testing with limited resources.

When faced with an insurmountable set of testing tasks (which is, really, always the case in testing), you may be tempted to begin at the beginning and see how far the testing progresses in the allotted time. Alternatively, you might pick and choose easy, quick tests across the entire feature set. Both approaches are convenient for the tester, but do they provide an adequate meal of testing?

To test well, testers must be aware of the constraints of finite tests, resources, and time. Testers must also be aware of their own personalities—the way they tend to attack the buffet.

Managers also must be aware of these constraints and tendencies. No matter how much you'd love the luxury, you can't expect testers to perform "exhaustive" tests. You'll have to reconcile yourself to satisfying your appetite for control in some other way.

Summary

There are an essentially infinite number of tests that can be performed on a particular product candidate. Rather than asking for "all" tests to be performed, managers and testers must strive to understand the risks added to the testing process by sampling.

Common Mistakes

1. *Demanding "test everything"*: When you demand the impossible, you have no idea what you'll get—except that it won't be anything impossible.

2. *Not understanding sampling:* Very few managers (very few people, in fact) understand sampling very well. Either educate yourself or hire an expert to audit your sampling. In either case, always be ready for the possibility of a sampling error.

3. *Spending too much for information that's not worth it:* Do you have a basement or garage full of expensive gadgets that you never really wanted? Do you realize what else you could have done with

the money spent (or the space occupied)? If so, you understand this error. Be careful what you ask for.

4. *Testing for the sake of appearance:* Some customers and certifying agencies demand "testing." You can go through the motions if you feel you must, but at least don't deceive yourself about the quality of the information you receive.

5. *Not using all sources of information:* Information gathered from test results is, by its very nature, limited, but there are other kinds of information sitting around if you're alert enough to see it.

6. *Thinking that machines can perform exhaustive testing, even if people can't:* It's not just the human brain that's limited; testing tools are limited, too. Don't buy any product that claims it can "perform all tests." Even if it could, you couldn't possibly look at all the results.

7. *Increasing risk by constraining resources:* When testing resources are cut, the easiest way to respond is by limiting sample size—running fewer tests. But with a reduced sample size, sampling errors become more likely. A diverse sample might find more problems than a large sample. Likewise, diversifying your test team might find more problems than enlarging your test team.

4

What's the Difference Between Testing and Debugging?

> *"Just definitions either prevent or put an end to a dispute."*
>
> —Nathanael Emmons, Theologian (1745–1840),
> as quoted in *The Works of Nathanael Emmons: With a Memoir of His Life*, ed. Jacob Ide (Boston: Crocker & Brewster, 1842).

The practice of testing has often received a bad reputation because of confusion over exactly what it is and what it's supposed to do. If a manager wants to make any progress understanding and improving testing, he or she is going to have to clarify the process. Paradoxically, that clarification may be more difficult if the manager has a great deal of experience developing software. Let's see how this works.

Early in her career, Jane, a project manager, was a one-woman development and support team in a tiny software consulting company that wrote custom applications for small businesses. Her job required that she wear many hats. Sometimes Jane was a programmer, creating the code that made up a product. At other times, she tested her code, making sure it did everything she intended and nothing she didn't. At still other times, she took calls from customers. On a typical day, Jane did all of these tasks, and that's where she learned the most about testing. Let's look back and travel with her through part of such a day.

Testing for discovery

At 8:56 A.M., Jane arrives for work. She gingerly places her Venti Caffè Latte on her desk, being careful not to spill it onto her

29

keyboard, then stows the salad she's brought for lunch and her bag under her desk. By 9:06, Jane has checked that the nightly code build went okay and that it launched the resulting executable version.

For the next half-hour, Jane runs through scenario after scenario, checking to see if her changes from the preceding day did what she expected without affecting any other functionality.

> Recap—Jane is *testing:* performing actions on the software under test that have the potential to discover new information.

Pinpointing

At 9:36 A.M., Jane encounters unexpected behavior. An update to the database didn't take. She reruns the same scenario. Sure enough, she's caught a bug.

> Recap—Jane is still *testing:* performing actions on the software under test that have the potential to discover new information. In this case, the new information is that the bug is repeatable. In determining that the bug is repeatable, Jane's also beginning another process.

What could be causing that? Jane wonders. She investigates further. *Is the bug repeatable with all updates or just updates that include optional fields? Does it matter what kind of data are in the updated field?*

> Recap—Jane is now *pinpointing:* isolating the conditions under which the bug occurs.

Locating

By 10:17, Jane knows that the bug only occurs when she's clearing optional fields. She opens the source code, sets a breakpoint, and begins stepping through the code that controls updates to the database.

> Recap—Jane is now *locating:* finding the location of the bug in the code so that she can fix it.

Determining significance

Fifteen minutes later, Jane has located the piece of code causing the problem. She sees that about fifty lines of code will have to be replaced if the update problem is to be removed. She thinks about how rarely this bug will be encountered in real use of the database. Since the repair of fifty lines carries certain risks, she weighs those risks against the risk of failing to update the database in certain circumstances. She decides this repair is significant enough to take the risk.

> Recap—Jane is now *determining significance:* balancing the risks of repairing versus not repairing this bug in the code.

Repairing

Jane spends a little time thinking about whether there are any less risky ways to fix the problem without changing the code, such as issuing a warning to users. She decides that a warning would not be sufficient protection, then spends some time thinking about various ways to repair the code: writing new code, patching the old code, copying similar code from another program, and so forth. She decides to patch the code and spends the next two hours doing so. Once she is finished, she repeats the test that first detected the bug and started the whole process—which may be called *debugging,* although this term is often used to mean *parts* of the process.

> Recap—Jane is now *repairing:* changing code to remove the problem.

Troubleshooting

At 12:46, Jane's phone rings. "Jane Chow," she answers as she pulls her salad out from under her desk and takes a small bite.

"Oh, I'm glad you're there!" The voice on the other end has a slight tinge of hysteria. Jane tries to place the voice. *Oh, yes, Sherman—over at Acme.*

"Sherman, good to hear from you. What can I do for you?" Jane tries not to roll her eyes and concentrates instead on spearing a forkful of tuna and tomato. *It's not Sherman's fault he's been asked to support Acme's software systems when his only prior computer experience was playing video games.*

"I need to restore something from backup and the system won't let me. Why isn't it working?"

Jane asks Sherman a series of questions: "Are you sure you have the right backup?" "Can you see the files through the operating system?" "What error did the backup software give you?" "Which recovery process are you using?" As Sherman answers, Jane remembers a bug in the backup routines that might be affecting Sherman's attempts to restore. She walks him through a different recovery process to see if that will work.

> Recap—Jane is *troubleshooting:* trying to remove and/or work around obstacles to make the software do what it's supposed to do.

Testing to learn

Jane finishes troubleshooting Sherman's problem at 1:40 P.M. and hangs up the phone. As she eats the last chunks of tuna, lettuce, and tomato, she checks her task list and sees that she has finished the work she'd scheduled for the morning—with twenty minutes to spare before her afternoon meeting. She reasons aloud, "Twenty minutes might be enough time to graph some statistics from my tests if I can just get this new graphics package to produce custom symbols." She's read the documentation and knows that it doesn't offer any straightforward explanation. She uses her twenty minutes to try out several theories about how custom symbols might work.

> Recap—Jane is testing again, but she's not trying to find bugs in the graphics package (although if she happens upon one, she'll report it). We could say she's *testing to learn:* an essential skill that might otherwise be called hacking, reverse engineering, or playing.

Task-switching

Jane easily shifts among activities—testing for discovery, pinpointing, locating, determining significance, repairing, troubleshooting, and testing to learn. As long as she continues to serve her customers, it doesn't really matter which task she performs at any given time.

However, in larger organizations with dedicated testers and/or customer support personnel, confusion about the differences among testing for discovery, pinpointing, locating, determining significance, repairing, troubleshooting, and testing to learn can lead to conflict, resentment, and failed projects.

What happens to testing as an organization grows?

Now let's switch to the present to look in again on Jane. We see that she has left the tiny software consulting company where she spent the early part of her career and has moved to a much larger firm as project manager for one of its commercial software products. This particular workday begins with the arrival of Stan, a software tester whose line-manager is Ken, one of the middle managers on Jane's project.

At his desk a few minutes before 8 A.M., Stan checks the bug database to see if there are any bug fixes for him to test. There's one bug in his queue, bug number 25073. *That's the one I filed yesterday,* he thinks. *They couldn't have fixed it that fast. It looked nasty.* He opens the record and discovers that the bug has been returned to him marked Need More Information. In the Programmer Comments section, Suni, the developer, has left a note: "Please test with all types of users, all backup options, and all display options, and tell me in which situations this occurs."

Stan found bug 25073 while testing and now Suni is asking him to pinpoint the exact conditions that trigger the bug. Sometimes pinpointing is part of the test group's job. Sometimes it isn't. More often than not, nobody specifies explicitly who is responsible for pinpointing. The testers assume that their job is to test (discover) while the developers assume that the testers' job is to support development—which to the developers means testing, pinpointing, and sometimes even locating or determining significance. Or even fetching coffee.

Fetching coffee? Yes, in some organizations, developers treat testers as if they're some kind of low-level gofers. When that kind of role-confusion happens, you can imagine how difficult it will be to create a sensible test-to-fix process. Stan, however, knows that no matter who is responsible for pinpointing, it's important to remember that pinpointing and testing are two different processes.

For the better part of the morning, Stan runs the different scenarios Suni has requested. At 11:33 A.M., just as Stan finishes pressing Submit on the bug form to return it to Suni with additional information, Stan's direct-line manager, Ken, stops by Stan's cubicle. "Hey, Stan, will you be able to get me those test results by noon like you promised?"

Stan looks at his watch. "Oh, crud. No. I just spent all morning working on that bug I told you about last night."

"I thought you filed that last night? What's to work on?"

Stan lets out a sigh. "Suni returned it to me to run a bunch of scenarios to get more information."

Ken stares at Stan, unable to believe what he is hearing. "That's not your problem. You had a reproducible case. You filed it. You were done." Seeing Stan's stricken expression, Ken eases off. "Okay, next time, come to me if a developer asks you to do that kind of work. Now please get me those test results before the end of today."

When Stan takes a mid-afternoon breather from preparing the test results for Ken, he re-checks his bug queue and finds 25073 is back, again marked Need More Information. Once again, Suni is asking him to run through a slew of scenarios to further pinpoint the bug. This time, however, Stan asks Ken whether he should do this for Suni, and receives a resounding "No" in response. Stan returns the bug to Suni with a note in the Comments section: "Sorry, no can do."

Instead of feeling relieved at having a clear understanding of his testing role, now Stan feels upset, torn between helping Suni and doing what his line-manager has asked him to do, but he isn't the only one on Jane's project who feels upset. Suni is upset because she thought Stan was there to help her. Ken is upset because all the time Stan spent pinpointing the bug for Suni was time he should have spent looking through the test results for new bugs. And Jane is upset because Ken's testing sub-team has disrupted her project's schedule.

The problem is that no one in the organization agrees to what extent testers are expected to pinpoint, so conflict is inevitable. The distinctions among testing for discovery, pinpointing, locating, determining significance, repairing, troubleshooting, and testing to learn become even more important when we are under pressure to speed up testing. Sometimes it's difficult to know exactly which one task we're doing. When we try to learn whether a bug is repeatable, for example, are we testing or pinpointing?

As a project manager with a high-level view of her interacting sub-teams, Jane can end the confusion as to who is responsible for what tasks by avoiding lumping these types of activities into one big blob labeled Testing. The only thing that lumping accomplishes is making the test process seem to take forever. But of course the actual testing—detecting failures—is only taking a fraction of the time accounted for under the general label Testing, and the fuzziness makes accurate estimating and scheduling impossible.

Since Jane's span of responsibility covers the test team, the development team, and the support team, she's the one who must clarify which people have primary responsibility for which tasks. Years ago, when she performed all these tasks herself, she didn't have to clarify which one she was doing at any time. But now, if she doesn't do this, there's no way she'll be able to improve her overall project and its likelihood for success.

Make the time-limit heuristic a management mantra—but adjust it as needed.

A heuristic that helps untangle who does what for how long states the concept simply:

> *Nobody on a project should carelessly waste the time of anyone on the project.*

Jane, in her role as project manager, applies this principle by teaching her testers to limit their time when investigating a bug to no more than ten minutes before alerting the programmer. Jane understands that what may be an obscure problem to Stan may be an obvious problem to the programmer, in which case Stan would be wasting his *own* time to consume more than ten minutes before seeking possibly more knowledgeable assistance.

Time-limiting is a heuristic principle, not a hard and fast rule. Stan uses many factors to adjust Jane's heuristic. For instance, if the programmer is five time zones away, Stan may investigate longer and batch his bug reports. There may be specific kinds of bugs that he has agreed to handle in specific ways—faster for some, slower for others.

Some test teams save developer time by having a dedicated bug investigator who lends a hand on any bug that requires more than a few minutes to lock down.

Another application of the principle is not wasting time making too-fine distinctions. For instance, there's no clear line between discovery and pinpointing that can be readily applied in all cases (or if there is one, I don't know of it). Rather than waste time arguing whether or not a specific activity is pinpointing, have both tester and developer pitch in and get the job done.

Summary

Many different tasks requiring many different skills are often lumped under the rubric Testing. Such lumping distorts planning, estimating, and job assignments, to the detriment of the entire project.

Common Mistakes

1. *Thinking that locating errors can be scheduled:* The only way we could know how long it would take to locate bugs would be to know where they are. If we know that, we wouldn't have to locate them at all.

2. *Not considering time lost to task-switching:* Task-switching can be beneficial, as we've seen, but like anything else, it has a cost. Each task-switch loses a bit of time, so if you're switching among about five tasks, you may be accomplishing nothing. Most people

react to that situation by simply dropping some of the tasks alto-gether, which can be dangerous.

3. *Treating testing as a low-priority task that can be interrupted for just about any reason:* Testing requires concentration if it's to be done reliably.

4. *Demanding that testers pinpoint every failure:* Testers can help developers with this job, if their time has been scheduled for it, but it is ultimately a developer responsibility. At least that's what I've seen work best in the long run.

5. *Demanding that testers locate every fault:* This is totally a developer's job, because developers have the needed skills. Testers generally don't have these skills, though at times, they may have useful hints.

6. *Repairing without retesting:* Repairs done in a hurry are highly likely to make things worse. If you're not in a hurry, you might be careful enough with the repairs not to need retesting, but if you're not in a hurry, why not retest?

7. *Ignoring cross-connections:* Commonly, the actions of programmers drive the need for testing, so that testing and programming are bound together. For instance, if programmers deliver code to testers late or in sub-par condition, then you'll have to adjust test expectations.

8. *Paying insufficient attention to testability:* Code that is designed and built to be testable can greatly reduce the time and effort associated with all aspects of testing.

9. *Insisting that all bugs be "reproducible":* Intermittent bugs need to be pursued with great vigor, not used as an excuse to delay testing or repairing. Use what information you have, and don't waste testers' time with unreasonable demands.

10. *Confusing testing with "creating and executing test cases":* Much of the testers' work is not captured or encapsulated within the confines of an identifiable test case. Consider thinking instead in terms of test activities.

11. *Demanding process overhaul in your company:* If you work in an organization that thinks it's the testers' job alone to pinpoint and locate bugs, or fetch coffee and donuts for the developers, you may now be tempted to confront your boss with a crass, revolu-tionary attitude. Even if you're interested in increasing respect for testers in your organization, you're not going to change the envi-ronment with rude demands. You might say to your boss, "I read

that a tester is someone who tries different methods in order to make things work. I've come to suspect our testers could do better work if some things were different here. I'd love to have some time to discuss these things with you."

5

Meta-Testing

"You can observe a lot by watching."
—Yogi Berra, Baseball Player and Manager (b. 1925),
and Dave H. Kaplan, *You Can Observe a
Lot by Watching* (Hoboken: Wiley, 2008).

The job of software testing, we know, is to provide information about the quality of a product. Many people believe that the only way to get such information is to execute the software on computers, or at least to review code. But such a belief is extremely limiting. Why? There's always other information about product quality just lying around for the taking—but only by managers who are watching, and who recognize it as relevant. [3]

Because of their psychological distance from a client's problems, external consultants are often able to see information that escapes the eyes and ears of their clients. Consider the following tale from my wife and partner, Dani Weinberg, about one of her consulting experiences in the dog-training world:

"A woman with a Sheltie puppy was at her wits' end because 'he always poops on the living-room rug.' She loved the little guy, so before giving up and taking him to the Humane Society, she came to me for a consultation. I listened to the woman describe the problem, then asked, 'Are there any other behavior problems?'

"The woman thought for a while, then said, 'Well, yes, there is one. He has this annoying habit of scratching on the front door and whining.'"

It's easy to laugh at someone else's inability to see the connection between two "problems," but that sort of blindness is typical of people who are too close, too emotionally involved with

39

a situation. Learning to recognize free information is one of the secrets of successful management of testing. You can learn quickly about the quality of an organization's products or the quality of the information it has obtained from machine testing.

Let's look at some more "Sheltie stories" from my own and others' consulting practices. Test yourself: See what information you can derive from them about the quality of a product or the quality of the information that's been obtained about the product through testing.

We have specs, but we can't find them.

I was asked to help an organization assess its development processes, including testing. I asked the test manager, "Do you use specs to test against?"

He replied, "Yes, we certainly do."

"May I see them?"

"You could," he said, "but we don't know where they are."

The inability to find key documents pretty much is Strike Three against an organization's development process. I didn't need a whole lot of details beyond this one piece of meta-information (information about the quality of information) to know that this organization was a mess, but I did continue by asking, "How long would it take you to find them?"

The test manager replied, "I don't know."

I then asked, "Okay, then how long will it take you to estimate how long it will take you to find them?"

To this he answered, "Maybe a month."

It turned out he was an optimist, but it didn't really matter. I had tested their testing process with a couple of simple questions.

We have so many bugs, our bug database doesn't work efficiently.

I was called in to help a product development organization's testing group. I learned that the testers were testing a product with about 40,000 lines of code.

"The problem," said the test manager, "is with our bug database."

"What's wrong with it?" I asked. "Is it buggy?"

"No, it's very reliable, but once it holds more than about 14,000 bug reports, its performance starts to degrade very rapidly. We need you to show us how to improve the performance so we can handle more bug reports."

These last two sentences add a treasure-trove of information. First of all, the testers think this is a database-performance problem when, at the very least, it's a problem with a development process that produces 14,000 bugs. That's probably all we need to know about their testing process, because no reasonable testing process was ever going to clear these bugs in any acceptable time—if it ever cleared them at all. (It turned out, development was producing more bugs faster than the existing bugs were being resolved, which was the next thing I investigated.)

The most important piece of information, in the end, was probably the lack of emotion with which the test manager reported these two sentences. Having a messed-up process is bad enough, but being clueless about that is much, much worse.

We didn't find many bugs, though we didn't really look.

Irene was asked to help improve the testing of a product with 22 components. The client identified "the worst three components" by the high number of bugs found per line of code. Irene asked which were the best components and was given the very low, bugs-per-line-of-code figures for each.

She then examined the configuration management logs and discovered that for each of these three "best" components, more than 70 percent of the client's code had not yet successfully been checked in for a build.

Here, we easily learn how clueless the client is about its measurement system, which is making the organization totally out of touch with what is really going on. They are flying blind—or worse—because they are using the wrong map. They have no idea how to measure quality, so they aren't likely to arrive at quality.

We modify our records to make bugs look less severe.

Linda was invited into a company to help the chief development manager evaluate his testing department's work. She started by looking at reports on the number and severity of bugs found each week. She noticed that the severity counts had been covered with white-out and written over. She scratched off each white-out and discovered that a higher printed number was under each highest severity count. Under each lowest severity count was a lower printed number. Puzzled, Linda asked the development manager for an explanation.

"Those are corrections by the product's development manager," he explained. "Sometimes the testers don't assign the proper severity, so the product development manager corrects them."

A moment's thought would show that this organization is always going to overestimate its progress toward a quality product. The fact that it hasn't spent a moment's thought is strong evidence that its trouble goes much deeper than simply falsifying records.

It's not in my component, so I don't record it.

I was watching a tester running tests on one component of a software product. As the tester was navigating to the target component, I noticed an error in one of the menus and pointed it out to the tester. The tester cursed and navigated around the error by using a direct branch.

I complimented the tester on his ingenuity and resourcefulness, then asked how he would document the error. "Oh, I don't have to document it," the tester replied. "It's not in my component."

This is another kind of falsification that will lead to overestimating progress toward a quality product, but I think it's likely to be even more serious than the previous case. That case involved one manager who was falsifying records. This case may prove to be a widespread attitude in the culture of the organization—a defect that will be much more difficult to uproot.

I'm testing the wrong application and don't know it.

Matt was asked to perform a participant-observation review in which he was constrained to observe testers at work without interfering in any way. He watched one tester spend the better part of several hours testing the scroll bars on a Web-based enterprise system. The scroll bars were, of course, part of the Web browser, not part of the system being tested.

It would be easy to dismiss this case as unfortunate information about the ignorance or low intelligence of a single tester, but there's more to it. Why is this tester allowed to go on so long on a task that should have been accomplished in a few minutes? Where is the supervision? Or, perhaps more serious, Where is the training? Where is the selection process for testers? Behavior like this is a symptom, so we need to ask a most important question: What's the disease behind it?

We don't test the worst components because it takes too long.

Called in to evaluate an organization's process, I asked the development manager whether the developers on her project unit-tested their code.

"Absolutely," she said. "We unit-test almost all the code."

"Almost all?" I asked. "Which code don't you unit-test?"

"Oh, some of the code is late, so of course we don't have time to unit-test that or we'd have to delay the start of systems test."

Here we see a sign of an oblivious manager, as well as that manager's manager's lack of attention. Why is nobody asking why certain code is late? If they asked, they would find out that it's late because the developers had trouble making it work. If any code was to be tested most thoroughly, it ought to be the latest code. Here, management has things backwards. What else, I wonder?

We found so many bugs, there couldn't be any more.

One of Melinda's clients conducted an all-day BugFest during which developers earned cash rewards for finding bugs in their latest release candidate. They found 282 bugs, which convinced them they were "close to shipping."

The client was so happy with the results that it repeated the event on the Saturday before the next release date. This time, the developers found 343 new bugs and excitedly announced that finding so many bugs indicated that they were "on the verge" of shipping.

The number of bugs found might be an indication of the state of the system, and we could use this information to see—as the client doesn't—that this system is in poor shape. But the most important clue here is that the client is clueless about the relationship between bugs found and bugs remaining. What else doesn't it know?

Our tests proved the program was correct.

Consulting with a general manager who was on the carpet because a recently shipped product was proving terribly buggy in the hands of customers, I asked him why he had allowed the product to ship. Without any hint of irony, he replied, "Because our tests proved that it was correct."

General managers don't need to know a great deal of detail about testing, but they do need to know that no amount of testing will ever "prove" a program is "correct." They also need to know that "correct" isn't even a definable concept. How come the testing organization hasn't educated its management even to this simple extent?

We ran so many test cases that we couldn't look at them all.

Another manager claimed to Raj that he knew his product was ready to ship because "we've run six-hundred-thousand test cases and nothing crashed the system." (Notice the second fallacy here: Anything that doesn't crash must be okay.)

This statement reveals in several ways that the speaker has no idea what testing is all about. Moreover, he thinks he knows, so that if he's managing the testing operation, the testers will be doing a great deal of meaningless work, which he'll reward.

If our software works okay for three users, obviously it will work okay for a hundred.

When I asked several testers about scheduling performance testing, they replied, "We've already done that."

"Really?" I said. "What exactly have you done?"

"Well, we ran the system with one user, and the response time was about ten milliseconds. Then we ran it with two users, and the response time was twenty milliseconds. With three users, it was thirty milliseconds."

"Interesting," I said. "But the system is supposed to support at least a hundred simultaneous users. So what response time did you get when it was fully loaded?"

"Oh, that test would have been too hard to set up, and anyway, it's not necessary. Obviously, the response time would be one second—ten milliseconds per user times one-hundred users."

This group of testers was committing The Linearity Fallacy (a form of The Composition Fallacy, which assumes that two small systems joined together make just twice as big a system, but no more). It is fact that if you have ten kilograms of pure uranium-235 and you add another ten kilograms, you'll have twenty kilograms. But if you do this a few more times, you won't have fifty kilograms, you'll have a nuclear explosion. One plus one doesn't always equal two. [4]

But the people in this organization don't understand The Composition Fallacy, so I would predict that their testing situation will grow worse and worse as their system grows bigger. And it will grow bigger, because they won't understand what kind of explosion they're getting into.

We don't want our testers to know we're ignoring their information.

A client I had just started working with called an emergency meeting to find out why testing was holding up product shipment. In the meeting, the testers presented fifteen failed tests that showed that the product did not even build correctly, so it couldn't be tested. They discussed each of the problems with the developers. After the meeting, the development lead wrote an e-mail summary of the meeting reporting that only two "significant" problems had to be solved prior to ship.

The e-mail was sent to the development manager, the marketing manager, and to each of the developers who attended the meeting. Not one of the testers who had presented the failed tests at the meeting was included in the cc-list, so none of them even knew that the e-mail was sent.

Here managers are not only falsifying information, they're withholding information from people who need to know it to perform their jobs. But even worse, they're falsifying someone else's information, making it look as if the testers said one thing when they said another. This organization isn't going far—at least not far forward.

I don't report bugs, so the developer won't be angry with me.

Sara watched a tester uncover five bugs in a component, but instead of logging the bugs in the bug database, the tester went directly to the developer of the component and reported them to her orally. Sara asked why the tester didn't record the bugs, and he replied, "If I do that, she screams at me because it makes her look bad."

Emotions are the dominant factor in this organization, if this tester is typical. Management By Screaming is not generally a highly successful leadership tactic. And quite likely, this is typical behavior. We know that the developer's manager uses fear, too, or why would the developer be so afraid of looking bad?

We don't need to test that, because the developer is really good.

Dennis reviewed a client's test plan and noticed that there was no plan to test one of the components. When he asked the test manager (who was new to the company) why it was missing, he was told, "We don't need to worry about that. The development manager assures me that this developer is very careful and conscientious."

Quite likely there's fear in this organization, too, although nobody's saying so. What they are saying is, "We don't know the first thing about real human beings." But even if they actually had a developer who was this good, why aren't they using her to bring the rest of the developers up to her level?

Follow up on meta-information.

Fourteen stories, fourteen shades of black, white, or gray. I hope you were able to extract meta-information from these stories. If you are not convinced that you have succeeded, consider what each of them tells you (or, if not tells, *hints* to you) about the quality of the information gathered from testing—the accuracy, relevance, clarity, and comprehensiveness.

Remember, though, that these stories are merely hints for you to interpret. Perhaps the Sheltie that pooped repeatedly on the rug did so because he had some medical problem requiring a veterinarian's attention, not the behavior problem his owner suspected. Perhaps there's a nonobvious explanation behind each of these Sheltie situations for you to follow up on. Use the hints that are provided to validate your intuition—or find another interpretation. And, even if your intuition is right on target, you probably won't have an easy time convincing others that you're correct. You will have to gather other evidence, or other allies, to influence the people who can influence the situation.

When Dani asked the Sheltie's owner why she thought the puppy was whining at the front door, the woman said, "I think I've spoiled him. He just wants to go out and play all the time, but I have too much housework to do—especially since I spend so much time cleaning up the mess on the rug."

When a problem persists in spite of how obvious the solution is to you, you aren't going to be able to convince others to solve the problem until you find out how they are rationalizing away the evidence that's so apparent to you. In the next chapter, we look at how people immunize themselves against information, and what you can do about it.

Summary

You can greatly improve the efficacy of your testing, and lower your costs, if you learn to use meta-information—information about the quality of information.

Common Mistakes

1. *Believing that all relevant information is contained in test reports:* Even if all tests are reported, at least half the information you need won't be in them.

2. *Believing you can sit in your office and know what is going on with testing:* Reports should be validated by your own direct observation of how they have been conducted and what's behind them.

3. *Believing that tests can "prove" anything correct:* All a test can show is that something failed or didn't fail under specific conditions. James Bach puts it this way: "I'm not in the proof business; I'm in the evidence and inference business."

4. *Believing that the mere existence of documents has some value:* If you don't use them, they're worthless. If they are misleading and you use them, they can be worse than worthless.

5. *Allowing the list of bugs pending assessment/fixing/assignment to grow beyond human comprehension:* If you're not keeping up with bugs, morale will suffer and you'll fall further behind. Better to stop producing new bugs and clear up old ones. Everyone will feel better and work better. If necessary, you can declare bug amnesty: Remove all bugs from the bug database and send a notice to all issuers telling them to resubmit a bug if they're still concerned about it. If they remain concerned, add the bug back into the queue. When I did this with the 14,000-bug database, the reduction was enormous and the problem was solved.

6. *Blaming people so they feel motivated to hide bugs:* It's not an error unless it leaves the office. Every time someone falsifies a record, you lose information that could help you manage your project.

7. *Rewarding people for going through the motions:* To test effectively, people have to both concentrate and focus. Concentration without focus might look good, but accomplishes little.

8. *Not recording every identified failure:* Caught failures are just too valuable to be ignored. If they're not recorded, they're likely to be ignored. If they're ignored, you're throwing away money and time. Not recording failures to "save time" will have exactly the opposite effect on your schedule.

9. *Over-recording every identified failure:* Recording can be expensive. James Bach suggests a MIP strategy—whereby MIP

stands for *Mention In Passing*. For some bugs, James may not prepare an expensive, formal write-up, but instead puts the information in an e-mail, reports it orally to the developer, or mentions it in a meeting. My own preference is to assign the bug an identifier in the bug database, with at least a reference to it in the e-mail or conversation. Otherwise, it's all too easy to distort statistics by playing games about what gets recorded and what doesn't.

On the other hand, by raising the cost of reporting, you can greatly improve the likelihood that a tester will self-censor, so look for ways to save expense. For example, certain classes of bugs, such as internationalization issues or spelling errors, might be reported in a batch as one record, rather than as separate records.

10. *Letting emotions determine what is tested and reported:* If you're not careful, you'll encourage bullying and co-dependency. Software-building is tough enough already.

11. *Using phony models to assess progress:* The more bugs you find, the more you're going to find, not the other way around. There are no perfect developers, regardless of how good a game they can talk.

12. *Assuming the official process description is always followed reliably and correctly:* A process description is just that, a description. And, it's a description of an ideal process, not of what has actually been done. To assume it has been followed, in the absence of any system to assure that it has been, is foolhardy.

13. *Believing in objectivity:* All information is interpreted and therefore subjective to some degree. Be aware of the forces that influence the quality of the information you're using.

14. *Failing to review carefully any document produced using a template:* Templates ensure that the *form* of documents is standard. Such documents tend to look pretty, but often camouflage unreliable information.

6

Information Immunity

"An error does not become truth by reason of multiplied propagation, nor does truth become error because nobody sees it."
—Mahatma Gandhi, Statesman and Humanitarian (1869–1948), and Krishna Kripalani, *All Men Are Brothers* (New York: Continuum International Publishing Group, 2005).

Although the purpose of testing is to provide information, people often view the information as threatening. Consider the underlying fears reflected in the following comments:

Project Manager:	"With all these bugs, I won't make my schedule."
Developer:	"That stupid error shows people I'm not as good a programmer as I'd hoped to be."
Marketing Manager:	"This product is so full of bugs, it isn't going to sell very well, and I won't make my numbers."
Tester:	"My boss is going to bite my head off if I report this error this late in the game."

Because information can be so threatening, we've all developed an "immune system" that tends to protect us from information we don't want to hear. Information immunity can undermine all your best testing efforts because your message about bugs may fall on deaf ears. So what does a manager have to watch for? Some answers are revealed in the following section, which explores the role fear plays in the workplace. Later chapters show how to allay fears primarily by clearing up common misconceptions and myths.

We are afraid when our rules are threatened.

When we are afraid, we try to defend ourselves. We have many defenses available to us, and if one fails, we may try another. We don't always succeed in conquering our fear or dissipating its effects, but when we feel threatened, we instinctively defend.

FEAR is defined by author Tom Crum as an acronym for *Fantasy Experienced As Reality.* [5] Our imagination—our fantasy—tells us that something bad may happen. Sometimes it's right and sometimes it's wrong, but either way, we defend.

The family therapist and author Virginia Satir noted that we bring our defenses to the fore when our self-esteem is low and some interaction invokes a *survival rule,* the breaking of which leads us to a strong, fearful feeling about our personal safety. Testing is especially prone to provoking such survival rules. For example,

- If someone shows you a bug in your program, you may invoke your survival rule that says, "I must always be perfect."
- If you're trying to use a program and you can't make it work properly, you may invoke your survival rule that says, "I must never be stupid."
- If tests are turning up lots of bugs and a project is not finishing swiftly, you may invoke your survival rule that says, "I must always be on schedule" or "I must always meet my commitments."
- If you are a professional tester, you may find yourself constantly facing the survival rule, "If you can't say something nice, don't say anything."
- If you have the survival rule, "If I don't find problems, I'm not doing my job," you may start to find all kinds of (nitpicky) problems.

51

If you are someone who is not shy about sharing bad news, you may get a reaction from the recipient of your news that touches your survival rule, "Never make anybody angry."

In such situations, people are endlessly creative in constructing defenses. Psychologists have broken down these defenses into half-a-dozen categories: repression, rationalization, projection, displacement, overcompensation, and compulsiveness. We take a closer look at each of these defense behaviors in the following sections.

We repress the unacceptable.

Repression is denying or overlooking what we deem to be unacceptable thoughts, feelings, and memories—for example, while condemning another's late arrival, we overlook the fact that we have been late on similar occasions in the past. A well-known symbol of repressive behavior is the ostrich with its head in the sand: *If I don't see it, it doesn't exist.*

Every form of defensive behavior probably involves repression in some form or another. Take, for example, my colleague Ella's experience while beginning to familiarize herself with a client's application. Ella discovered that dragging text from a text box on the screen and dropping it in another window resulted in a crash. She figured the tester would want to know about the problem, so she stopped by his cubicle and said, "Hey, let me show you something." She then demonstrated what she'd found.

The tester stared at her for a few seconds and then replied. "Yeah?"

"Don't you think it's a bug?"

"No. Users shouldn't do that."

[To this point, the tester's reaction is more an example of displacement than repression, but then he continues, with a conscious repression.]

"And besides, the developers have enough bugs on their plate right now. I don't want to find more until they fix the ones they already know about."

In other words, *more bugs now* would be unacceptable, so there won't be any.

Repression can be conscious or it can be unconscious, as when people shade the truth to lead themselves or others away from perceived danger. Take, for example, a failure case that is submitted by a tester to a developer who dismisses it and writes, "This is not a bug, as mentioned in issue number 173." The tester recognizes that issue 173 doesn't mention this failure at all, and understands that if he simply accepts this statement, the bug will remain in the application, with the developer protected from doing anything about it. Was the bug consciously repressed, or unconsciously repressed? Does it matter?

Undoubtedly, the most common repression that testers hear from developers is "I didn't change anything." What this means is made clear by mentally adding the repressed part of the sentence, giving, "I didn't change anything that should matter, that I thought was important, except for what I did change." [6]

Often you can detect that repression defenses are in place by the strong emotions generated during a discussion between a tester and a manager. In the following, a tester represses a bug and a manager reacts:

> Manager: "Wasn't that a bug?"
> Tester: "No, it does that all the time. You just restart and it's okay."
> Manager: "Have you filed that as a bug?"
> Tester: "No, it's not a bug. It's just the way it is."
> Manager: "You must be kidding!"

When the manager described this exchange to me, more than a year had passed since it happened, but he was still so angry that he literally shook as he related the story.

We rationalize the unreasonable.

Rationalization is trying to make meaningless, stupid, or irrational actions appear reasonable—for example, a developer is rationalizing if he claims, "I really left mistakes in the program so we'd know if the testers were doing a good job."

Consider the following situation: A database query system designed for a client I visited in Arkansas had been structured so that there were two ways for users to log out—either by hitting a button or by using a menu. When a user logged out using the button, a "confirm log out" screen appeared, giving the user the option either to confirm log out or to cancel the command to stay logged in. When a user logged out using the menu, log out was immediate, with no option to cancel.

Testers thought the two log-out options should be consistent, but the developer disagreed, "This is a feature, because it gives the user two different ways to log out, one with confirmation and one without. Besides, I can't change it easily, so it's best if you accept it." In other words, if you can't fix it, feature it—a perfect example of rationalization, which sounds rational if you don't think too deeply about it. [7]

Not that testers are always rational. Developers often catch testers making irrational arguments, so not every push-back against a tester's report is an example of rationalization or some other pathology. In the case of the database query system, though, most people would agree that the developer's arguments are irrational and that the inconsistency between log-out methods is a problem, not a feature.

How could the tester appeal to the developer without increasing the perceived threat of the situation? He could start by first deconstructing the developer's defense (using logic such as is shown in Steps 1, 2, and 3, below), and then state that a fix needs to be devised (Step 4):

Step 1. "Users generally don't index different flavors of a feature in terms of buttons versus menu. That's not a typical design in graphical user interfaces."

Step 2. "Users generally expect that the application will behave in ways that can be undone, unless there is a warning message first (unless they have explicitly turned off 'confirmations' in the Options dialogue)."

Step 3. "Consistency is a major factor in improving the user's learning curve. This includes consistency within the application and consistency with other popular products."

Step 4. "We need to think of ways to implement the fix. If it is really so hard to fix, knowing that gives us meta-information about the likelihood of other important problems in development of this code."

The tester, however, shouldn't be surprised if these steps don't work. Usually, logical arguments don't change a position that wasn't arrived at by logic.

We project our own negative qualities onto other people.

Projection, when negative, is criticizing others for having the same qualities we dislike in ourselves—for example, if I secretly suspect that I am a bit selfish or overbearing, I might pick up on these negative qualities in another, complaining, "he's greedy" or "she's controlling." The following story demonstrates projection's invasive behavior.

Each time Missy, a tester in the Netherlands, enters a new value in the SEARCH field, her computer screen goes blank. Totally blank. After a minute, the screen is still blank. After an additional period of time that lasts between two and eight minutes, the screen lights up with the message SEARCH COMPLETE, and all the regular menus reappear.

Ken, the developer who operates out of London, explains the behavior to Missy when she contacts him: "This is not a bug. It just takes awhile to complete a search. There's a lot of stuff to check in there."

Missy says, "It's not a very good idea to have work proceeding and not let the user know. After a few minutes, the user may think the system has crashed."

Ken replies, "Programming a message to show that work is proceeding despite the blank screen would take me a lot of time. Then I'd have to wait more time, probably until after lunch, for the new build. I don't have that kind of time."

"But it's important," Missy argues. "The first several times I tried this, I thought the system had crashed. I tried hitting some keys, and then it did crash."

"Well," says Ken, "you and all the other users just have to learn to be patient. You have to appreciate the amount of work the program is doing."

Here, the impatient developer projects his own impatience onto all users, thus defending himself from having to admit that he didn't do a perfect job designing the code.

The issue was closed as "not a bug." It turned out that as the system was used and more and more data were entered, the delay grew longer and longer, with no apparent upper limit. Do you think the users' patience increased to accommodate the application? It's "not a bug" only if the users are more patient than Ken.

We displace blame to absolve ourselves.

Displacement is blaming someone or something that's not the real source of our troubles, thereby absolving ourselves of responsibility—for example, "my pencil broke, so I couldn't finish my homework." Displacement is vividly illustrated in the following testing story from Japan, reported by the tester as "three steps that crash a system":

1. Go to the ADD USER page.
2. Keep adding users until you try to add the sixty-fourth user.
3. Discover that the screen now displays an "out of memory" error message and the system hangs, needing a cold restart.

Upon being contacted by the tester, the developer says, "You're only allowed sixty-three users. That's for performance reasons, so this is actually a feature that helps the administrator stay out of trouble."

The tester says, "Don't you think there is a more gracious way to keep administrators out of trouble than by crashing the system?"

[Up to this point, the developer's statement has been a rationalization, but it quickly turns as he switches his defensive strategy to displacing the blame onto the users.]

The developer replies, "They should know they aren't allowed more than sixty-three users. Anyway, after a few crashes, they'll learn. Smart people learn fast not to do things that make the system crash."

Putting the blame on the users is especially ludicrous when viewed in the light of the preceding story because the particular user list wasn't numbered and could only be seen in a fixed window that showed three-and-a-half users at a time. Probably not too easy to learn from.

In any case, developers can't control what "smart" people will learn. Perhaps users will learn to assume that the product could crash and lose data at any moment. Perhaps they will learn to avoid using this product at all. Perhaps they will learn the merits of working with a competing product.

Following are some common displacement complaints we hear when a developer is faced with an unacceptable problem from a tester. First, there is displacement onto the tester:

- *"If you can't reproduce it, I can't do anything about it."*
- *"You're being too picky."*

If there's no obvious tester involved, a developer may displace blame and fear onto other developers:

- *"It's* their *code."* ("Their" often refers to a third party's software, or—perhaps even more often—to code written by a programmer or developer who has left the organization.)
- *"It's not* my *code."* (Somebody out there is to blame, but certainly not me.)

Developers may also displace blame and fear onto their managers:

- *"They think new features are more important than working features, so I'm putting in new features now."*
- *"I have to go to too many management meetings, so I don't have time."*

Developers may even displace blame onto the universe at large:

- *"It's a limitation of the system. All systems have limitations."*
- *"That's just the way the world works."*
- *"Software is like that."*
- *"The [infrastructure component] [operating system] [network] doesn't allow that."*

We overcompensate for our self-perceived deficiencies.

Overcompensation is exaggerating our attempts to compensate for some real or imagined personal deficiency—for example, a man becomes a workaholic because he feels he's unlovable. The following came to me from a client in Canada and tells the story of Avery, an overcompensating tester:

Avery tested an administrative tool that configured backups. When creating his test cases, he forgot to include cases that tested backups to CDs. When this omission was pointed out, Avery overcompensated by creating test cases for more than 140 different pieces of hardware to which backups *might* be made—including paper tape, which hadn't been used in decades.

We become compulsive when we feel we're losing control.

Compulsiveness is being unable to depart from a counterproductive behavior pattern—for example, a person is incapable of allowing small deviations from a defined process. An example from one of my British clients shows the damaging effects of compulsiveness:

Valerie, a developer, finds a way to insert a patch in the build, bypassing the configuration management system. Nigel, the tester, finds a fault in the patch, which crashes the system.

Valerie says, "The problem shouldn't be entered in our tracking system. I never put the patch in the configuration management system, so it's not an official bug. I was just trying something out."

Nigel recognizes that Valerie's comment is a rationalization. He responds quickly, "Yes, but our process requires that anything that goes into the system must go through configuration management so it can be tracked."

Valerie replies with an edge in her voice, "Okay, next time I want to try something out, I won't patch the system. Either I'll put it in the configuration management system, or I'll try it out on a system of my own."

"Absolutely not," insists Nigel. "Developers are not allowed to try things out."

"And why not?" demands Valerie, frowning.

"I've checked the process manual. There's nothing in it that permits trying things out," says Nigel, sensing that he is losing control, perfectly illustrating defense by compulsion.

What's Nigel afraid of? When questioned, he replied, "If we start making exceptions, I'll lose control of everything that's going on here." Of course, he's really not in control in the first place, but he has a rule that says, "I must always be (feel) in control." Valerie's behavior challenges his rule.

If we want to delve deeper into Nigel's psyche, we might discover that what he's really doing is repressing and displacing. Perhaps he's attracted to Valerie, but represses the feeling as inappropriate, shutting it out of his conscious awareness. If this is the case, it's no wonder that whenever she comes around, he feels he might lose control of himself. To maintain control, he displaces that feeling by pushing blame onto Valerie and all the other developers in all other situations.

Summary

Information is neutral, but people's reactions to information are rarely neutral. To assess testing information, you must take into account people's emotional defenses—repression, rationalization, projection, displacement, overcompensation, and compulsiveness. By remaining vigilant, thoughtful, and pragmatic, you can help diffuse emotional chaos and prevent illogical processes from undermining your testing efforts.

Common Mistakes

1. *Failing to notice when people are fearful:* Defense mechanisms are usually easy to spot if you're looking for them.

2. *Creating a fearful environment:* If you blame messengers for bringing news you don't want to hear, you'll be rewarded by not hearing the news you should hear.

3. *Allowing your fears to override the facts when making decisions:* To succeed in the software business, you need to be aware of your own rules and how they distort your intake of information.

4. *Allowing your hopes to override facts when making decisions:* It's all right to hope for anything, but hoping is not the same as *expecting* anything. [8]

5. *Indulging in compulsive behavior:* One person's compulsiveness frequently engenders fear and defensiveness in others. Your first priority should be to strive to be reasonable.

6. *Assuming that any argument against your own point of view is part of a pathology:* In the same way that a rationalization can sound like a good argument, a good argument can sound like a rationalization. Many people are uncomfortable making arguments. Many are untrained in the art of persuasion. Learn to listen sympathetically to objections and justifications. Try to find and honor what's worthwhile in an opposing viewpoint—there's almost always something there to value.

For instance, the argument "It's too hard to fix that" might be the speaker's way of saying, "I don't know how to fix that quickly or cheaply, and I'm not convinced doing so would be a good way to use my time." This may indeed be true. Perhaps it's worth talking about.

7. *Outright denial:* The test consultant and writer Pradeep Soundararajan sent me a wonderful story illustrating how far a person can go in denying facts: At a company he worked for in India, the developers had a habit of saying "Works As Designed," or WAD, to reject a bug. When he reported a bug that caused a freeze of the screen, the developers closed the bug, marking it as WAD. He was surprised, to say the least. It's rather unusual for a screen freeze to be part of a product design.

He needed the developers to explain WAD, asking, "Do you know the design so well or refer to it? Could you point me to that design document?"

A developer replied, "Well I don't know where it is, but I understand it very well because that's what I was reading for an entire month after I joined here." (It was more than a year since he had joined.) "Moreover," he continued, "you are a contract tester. Design documents are confidential, so we can't show it to you."

7. *Thinking it can't happen here:* I intentionally chose examples for this chapter from around the world to show that these defenses are universal human responses. They can happen anywhere.

7

How to Deal With Defensive Reactions

> *"No passion so effectually robs the mind of all its powers of acting and reasoning as fear."*
>
> —Edmund Burke, British Statesman and Orator (1729–1797),
> *A Philosophical Enquiry into the Origin of Our Ideas of the Sublime and Beautiful,* ed. Adam Phillips
> (New York: Oxford University Press, 1998).

You don't have to be a psychologist to deal more effectively with defensive reactions that make people immune to important information. Imagine, for a moment, that you are our British tester Nigel's manager and you notice that he's being compulsive about enforcing rules. It's not your business to know why, but merely to correct the situation by establishing reasonable rules and guidelines. Perhaps Nigel will respond to a new "rule" that says, "Everything that's not explicitly forbidden is allowed."

It's not only not necessary to be a psychologist, it's not a good idea to play one, either. People sometimes get defensive, especially when they feel unjustly accused of being defensive. In fact, accusation of defensiveness is a popular way to try to marginalize a person's contribution to a debate. Don't play that game. It destroys information.

In any case, how would you know that a reaction is defensive? Even if you were a licensed psychologist, you couldn't *know,* but there are some heuristics that help. For instance, does the reaction seem out of proportion to its ostensible cause?

The most useful heuristic is first not to label the reaction as defensive, but then treat it as if it were and see if it yields to gentle tests.

Identify the fear.

From the outset, you need to understand that fear drives defensive reactions—although the underlying fear will generally not be visible to you. Nevertheless, it's there. See whether you can identify what a person fears, then see what happens when you find a way to reduce that fear.

Testers' defenses, like everyone else's, can immunize them to unpleasant information. Let's look at the defense I see testers evince most often: "You don't care about quality." Suppose it's late in the afternoon on the last day when product changes are allowed and Nigel, our tester in Britain, finds a grammatical error in an obscure error message in one of Valerie's programs. The message could occur only in configurations that have a rare model of attached disk drive (estimated to be the case for fewer than one customer in 10,000). Furthermore, the message could occur only if the user activates a feature of the system that only one percent of the users would ever be likely to need. A user who meets all these criteria would see the message: ONE OR MORE ERROR IN INPUT STRING.

When the problem is pointed out to Valerie, she acknowledges that the afflicted part of the message should have read "ONE OR MORE ERRORS" not "ONE OR MORE ERROR." Nigel's manager recommends that they classify the severity of the problem as "cosmetic," stating that it's not worth risking a last-minute change. At that recommendation, Nigel flares up, shouting at his manager "You don't care about quality!" If you were Nigel's manager, what would you do?

Use critical thinking.

This is one of many areas where critical thinking and testing meet. Some defenses—in the critical thinking sense of the word—are invalid arguments. This one, for example, is what logicians call an ad hominem (at the person) attack. But if Nigel didn't arrive at this defense through logic, then no amount of logic is going to persuade him to drop it. Therefore, the helpful way to use logic in such a situation is to find out if Nigel's argument is based on logic or not.

Rather than responding in kind and angrily telling Nigel to take a hike, which would be very un-British, Nigel's manager could ask, "What do you mean by quality?" If Nigel agrees with this book's definition of quality—value to some person—the point could be clarified by his manager asking him, "What value will be lost to what person if we don't fix this error in today's release?" In Nigel's answer, his manager could quickly discover whether Nigel bases his argument on logic or pure and simple fear.

For instance, if Nigel does not respond logically to his manager's perfectly logical and reasonable question, we might conclude that Nigel is motivated by factors other than the quality of the product. Perhaps Nigel *does* have a crush on Valerie and is looking for an excuse to work late with her. Or perhaps he was once hit on the knuckles by his teacher for not using a plural. Whatever the case, it doesn't matter. It's nobody's business (unless Nigel has behaved in ways that are discriminatory or illegal, such as harassing coworkers, when such behavior does become the business of personnel and legal advisors).

What *is* your business as manager is shipping a valuable product in a timely manner. So, you point out to Nigel that fewer than one customer in a million can possibly be affected by this mistake, and, if affected, is unlikely to be troubled by it. You contrast this loss of value with the chance that every customer might be affected if fixing this mistake at the last minute, late in the night, results in another problem. And then you go ahead and classify the mistake as "cosmetic—not to be corrected in this release."

If Nigel keeps on objecting, days and weeks later, you know that something else is going on, something fearful—to him. Watch for patterns, and eventually you may uncover the root cause of fear. If not, you'll eventually decide whether or not Nigel is worth the bother of his constant and compulsive blaming. Then you act accordingly.

Practice, practice, practice.

With sufficient practice, you'll grow much better at recognizing defensive reactions and dealing with them. Some of them are so common that you'll hear them repeatedly, such as,

"It's for the user's own good."

"It works the way I designed it."
"It's too [risky] [costly] [hard] to fix."
"No one will [notice] [care]."
"There's a workaround."

What makes these defenses effective is that there's some truth in each of them, some circumstances in which they might be rational, not rationalizations. If they didn't have that germ of rationality, they'd be easy to dispense with, as when a tester screamed at me, "What could you possibly know about this? You've never tested assembly-language programs."

Considering the fact that I first wrote and tested assembly-language programs twenty-five years before this screamer was born, it was rather easy for me to identify this defensive reaction as *not* arising from logic or reality.

Test yourself.

As you finish reading this chapter on managing defensive reactions, try testing yourself. If you had been in my place when the mad assembly-language tester screamed at me, how would you have responded? Or, practice on how you would respond to the following situation described to me by a fellow consultant:

Test:
1. Lower the virtual memory to the minimum needed to run the OS.
2. Launch a document in the application.
3. Edit the document.
4. Save the document.
Result:
5. Crash, requiring reboot of the entire system.

When given the bug report, the developer responded, shaking his head vigorously, "Oh. That's not a bug."

"What do you mean 'that's not a bug'? It crashes."

"Look," shrugged the developer. "It can crash or it can corrupt your data. Take your pick."

This is the common defensive reaction we call "It could be worse." And, yes, it could be worse. This might be the best developer in your organization.

Summary

If you start out properly and remain vigilant, thoughtful, and proactive, you can prevent emotional chaos from dominating your testing effort.

Common Mistakes

1. *Failing to take differences into account:* Everybody has rules. Everybody has fears when their rules are threatened. But the rules are different, and so are the reactions. You must treat everyone equally, but not necessarily in the same way.

2. *Telling people they don't care about quality:* Pretty much everybody cares about quality, although they may not understand how to produce it. Or, they may know how to produce quality that's consistent with *their* notion of quality, but not with yours. Don't insult them; teach them. In particular, teach them that different people can have different, valid perceptions of quality— and teach them which perceptions count in this particular situation.

3. *Leaving your brain outside:* If you believe that you're in such an emergency that you can't afford to think about errors, you might as well quit right now.

4. *Being overcritical of yourself:* It takes practice to learn to recognize and deal effectively with defensive reactions. Cut yourself a little slack if you make some mistakes.

5. *Not being critical of yourself:* If you are a manager, it's your job to deal with people's reactions that interfere with their doing their job. If you're not improving at this skill, then you're not doing *your* job. What's getting in your way?

8

What Makes a Good Test?

"There is nothing either good or bad,
but thinking makes it so."

—William Shakespeare, English Dramatist and Poet
(1564–1616), *Hamlet,* Act 2, Scene 2.

What makes a good test? The question can be answered at a highly technical level, but that's not our goal here. In fact, it's helpful to step back from that debate and look at the question from a management point of view. How can you know if testing is being done well? How much credence can you put in test results?

You can never know for sure.

You may or may not agree with Hamlet that there is nothing either good or bad. For the sake of argument, though, let's suppose there is such a thing as a "good" test and ask the question, How can one know whether a particular test (or set of tests) is, indeed, good?

Let's start with something even better than "good" by looking at a definition of "perfect." A perfect set of tests would have the following characteristics:

    a. It would detect every bug in a system.
    b. It would never detect a non-bug as a bug.
    c. It would give us complete confidence that it has done *a* and *b.*
    d. It would accomplish *a, b,* and *c* quickly and cheaply enough for our needs.

Now consider a system under test. In the simplest case, if that system were perfectly bug free (a situation likely to exist only in our dreams), then any test that finds no bugs meets condition *a*. Some tests that we would consider really lousy could meet that condition as well, but when run against a bug-free, *perfect* system, they would look pretty good.

Or would they? We don't know in advance whether we're testing a bug-free system or a louse-y system. (If we did, why would we need to test?) So, imagine two sets of tests: perfect tests and lousy tests. When run against our bug-free, perfect system, both sets of tests reveal no bugs. So, on the basis of their bug-finding alone, we couldn't tell the difference between a perfect test and a lousy test.

In fact, what might be an adequate test for one implementation of a system might be a lousy test for another implementation of the same system. In other words, "goodness" cannot be a property of a test, but only a property of the relationship between a test and an implementation.

Going one step further, the same test of the same implementation might be adequate for one organization but lousy for another. For example, a test that is adequate for a system to be used internally by a single organization might be totally inadequate if the same implementation were sold as a software product to a thousand organizations. In other words, "goodness" cannot be a property of tests *and* implementations, but only a property of the *relationship* among tests, implementations, and situations.

So, you can never tell for sure, and you never can tell by looking at a test in isolation, whether a test is good—but you do have many ways to tell whether a test is likely to be bad. Meta-tests play an important role. Later, in Chapter 9, we examine some indicators of "bad" tests.

You can assess goodness only after the fact.

If you knew how many bugs were in a system, you could at least begin to assess the goodness, or not-badness, of a set of tests. For instance, after a system has been in use for a few years, a prudent manager will have statistics on how many bugs were shipped with the system. By keeping track of what bugs turn up in use, then analyzing them to see what they're like, you will have at least some kinds of information, such as,

- *how good your testing was, and in what ways*
- *how testing might be improved in the future*
- *what kinds of bugs your testing characteristically missed*

Knowing such information allows you to make better estimates in the future, even if you don't improve your testing process. Such information may also be used to improve the development process—although in this regard, most likely I'm dreaming again.

Unfortunately, you never know for sure how many bugs were shipped because bugs can turn up in a product many, many years later, or never. Thirty years after I wrote *The Psychology of Computer Programming*, and after more than 200,000 copies of the published book had been sold, I received a letter documenting an "obvious" error that nobody else has ever pointed out to me. That was a useful lesson in author humility, but it also suggests that similar "obvious" errors can remain dormant in products—especially when the product is software—for a very long time. Software may even have bugs that were not bugs when the system shipped, such as functions that fail when an application is used with new hardware or a new operating system.

Moreover, if you wait five years to assess the goodness of a set of tests, what good is the information? Your testers, if they're still around, probably now use different tools and techniques. You may not have the original source code or bug reports, or you may have them and be unable to read or understand them. But if you wait only six months or a year, and keep good records, you may be able to assess the quality of a set of tests in time for the assessment to be useful in improving future tests.

Can you do better than simply waiting for experience? You can review your coverage and your oracles against your theories of failure. You can vary your tests randomly or arbitrarily and notice how problems emerge. You can compare different kinds of testing in parallel, such as beta testing compared to internal testing, or reviews compared to dynamic testing.

You may want to insert bugs intentionally.

Sometimes, you can gain quantitative estimates of how many problems might remain in software by seeding (or "bebugging," a term I believe I coined—and wrote about—in *The Psychology of Computer Programming).* Insert known bugs without telling the testers, then estimate the number of remaining unknown bugs by the percentage of known bugs they find.

For bebugging to work at all reasonably, the distribution of inserted bugs must closely match the (unknown) distribution of the unknown bugs. What I learned to do was leave (but document secretly) bugs that were made naturally but had been found by the developers, perhaps in code reviews, perhaps in unit testing. This gives the bugs a naturalness, but of course isn't necessarily a reliable sample of not-found bugs. Still, the practice provides some information if some known bugs aren't found. Be careful, though—it doesn't give a great deal of reliable information even if *all* the known bugs are found.

Estimates of goodness are always statistical.

In the end, though, an estimate of goodness is just that—an estimate. We can only estimate goodness statistically, because we can never know for sure how many bugs are, or were, in a given system. The fewer bugs there actually are in a system, the more the statistics are in our favor. For example, if there are ten bugs, a 50-percent error means we might be off by five bugs, but for 14,000 bugs, we might be off by 7,000.

To make your testers look good, you may want to come into test with as few bugs as they can reasonably manage. As an added benefit, testers are free to look for the difficult bugs if they aren't spending time finding the easy ones—noise that should have been removed during unit testing. Unfortunately, many managers judge testers by how many bugs they find, which means that poor-quality systems make testers look better. If they were testing a perfect system, they'd never find any bugs, and probably would be fired as incompetent. Under such a system of measurement, a lousy developer is a tester's best friend.

Why, then, is this flawed system so popular? One reason is the testers' lack of effort to explain how they look for bugs and why their strategy should inspire respect. Another reason is that when managers and developers *assume* that a product works, telling them it works seems to provide no information. That is, "no information" seems to equal "no value." It's the same reason why people don't replace the batteries in their smoke alarms—most of the time, a nonfunctioning smoke alarm is behaviorally indistinguishable from one that works. Sadly, the most common reminder to replace the batteries is a fire.

You can estimate not-badness.

At its deepest technical level, testing involves some rather esoteric mathematics and logic. To assess whether these esoteric activities have been done well, most managers must rely on second and third opinions from independent experts. There are, however, many assessments of not-badness most managers can make themselves by answering the following kinds of questions:

- *Does testing purport to give me the information I'm after?* If it doesn't, it's obviously not good.
- *Is it documented?* If not, have you personally observed the testing, or is it observed, reported, or performed by someone you trust?
- *Is it honest?* There are numerous ways test documentation can be fudged, intentionally or unintentionally.
- *Can I understand it?* If you can't, how can you possibly know whether it's good or bad?
- *Does it at least cover what matters most?* You can't generally test every path (remember the impossibility of exhaustive testing), but at the very least, a set of tests should visit each line of code once.
- *Is it actually finished?* Anyone can check a box on a test plan. Do you have ways of knowing what was actually done?
- *Can I tell the difference between a test and a demonstration?* Demonstrations are designed to make a system look

good. Tests should be designed to make it look the way it truly is.

- *Are trends and status reports overly simplistic and regular?* In real projects, tests and test activities come in many sizes and shapes. If test status reports show extremely predictable trends, testing may be shallow or the reports may be leaving out something important.
- *Are there inconsistencies between different kinds of test activities?* For instance, if beta testers find bugs that the internal test team doesn't find, or if performance testing finds functional bugs, that may be a sign that one or the other process is not working well.
- *Are managers visible?* They shouldn't hang over people's shoulders, but often testing can be improved simply by the presence of a curious manager who is known for paying attention.

Unfortunately, many fallacies and falsifications can distort tests, causing testing to turn sour. Managers need to understand and guard against them, possibly by applying methods detailed in the next several chapters.

Summary

You'll never know for sure whether your testing was done well, but there are many ways to know or estimate if it was done badly.

Common Mistakes

1. *Not thinking about what information you're after:* Testing is difficult enough when you *do* think about what you're after, and more or less impossible when you don't. You won't often know in advance what information you seek—in fact, in most instances, you'll have only an approximate idea. So, you need to think about your ultimate testing goals and about how you're going to *learn* what *other* information you're going to want.

2. *Measuring testers by how many bugs they find:* Testers will respond to this kind of measurement, but probably not the way you intend them to. The quantity of bugs found will increase, but the quality of information harvested will diminish.

3. *Believing you can know for sure how good a test is:* Be vigilant and skeptical when evaluating the accuracy and appropriateness of a test. If you aren't, you're going to get slapped down by the nature of the universe, which doesn't favor perfectionism.

4. *Failing to take context into account:* There are few, if any, tests that are equally significant in all circumstances. If you don't take potential usage patterns into account, your tests will be ineffectual.

5. *Testing without knowledge of the product's internal structure:* There are an infinite number of ways to replicate specific behavior on a finite series of tests. Knowing about the structure of the software you're testing can help you to identify special cases, subtle features, and important ranges to try—all of which help narrow the inference gap between what the software can do and what it will do during actual use. Charles Babbage, the maker of the very first computer, knew this almost 200 years ago, so there's no reason for you not to know it.

6. *Testing with too much knowledge of the product's internal structure:* It's too easy to make allowances for what you think you know is going on inside the black box. Typical users probably won't know enough to do that, so some of your tests had better simulate activities likely to be performed by naïve users.

7. *Giving statistical estimates of bugs as if the numbers were fixed, certain numbers:* Always give a range when stating the estimated number of bugs (for example, say, "There are somewhere in the range of thirty to forty bugs in this release."). Even better, give a statistical distribution, or a graph.

8. *Failing to apply measures of "badness" to your tests:* Use a checklist, asking questions such as the ones in this chapter.

9. *Not ensuring that development is done well:* Poorly developed code needs good testing but usually receives poor testing, thus compounding problems. What use are good tests of shoddy code?

10. *Not considering the loss of testing efficiency caused by numerous found bugs:* A "perfect" testing session is one entirely dedicated to test design and execution (this is the exception, not the rule). Set-up, bug investigation, and reporting take time away from test design and execution. Finding lots of bugs might make testers look good, but finding lots of bugs slows down testing, reduces coverage, or both.

73

9

Major Fallacies About Testing

> *"An expert is a person who avoids small error as he sweeps on to the grand fallacy."*
>
> —Benjamin Stolberg, Writer and Public Figure (1914–1951),
> as quoted in Ralph Woods, *The Modern Handbook of Humor for Speakers, Writers, Business and Professional Men and for All Who Enjoy Sharing Humor with Others* (New York: McGraw-Hill, 1967), p. 14.

There may be an infinite number of ways of doing testing badly, but there are a few very fallacious ways of thinking that can ruin any testing project. Let's start our exploration of why bad testing occurs by looking at some fallacies in action.

The Blaming Fallacy

Kahn, a project manager at Able Corporation, sinks into his chair and sighs. The day has not gone well, and he is in a foul mood. It started on his way into the building first thing in the morning when Randolph, the top salesman, gave him an earful about some irate customers. Over lunch, Kahn's boss ever so politely chewed him out about a huge sale the company lost due to quality issues. *Why doesn't she just come right out and say what's on her mind?* Kahn thinks. *A polite chewing out is still a chewing out, and if she could just get to the point, it would be over faster!*

Kahn's boss and Randolph seem to think that if they point the finger of blame and speak using a blaming tone and volume, problems will get solved more quickly, effectively, and efficiently. They subscribe to The Blaming Fallacy.

In fact, the opposite is generally true: The more time and effort someone spends looking for someone else to blame for a problem, the less the chance of solving the problem. Fallout from The Blaming Fallacy is quite common: Kahn will pass the blame on to the first vulnerable person he sees. In this case, that person is Rose, his new test manager, who just now knocks on his office door. "You want to see me?"

"Rose! Good! You got my voicemail." Kahn pulls himself out of his reverie and assesses his new test manager. *She'll be okay once I break her in,* he tells himself. "Come in," Kahn says. "You need to do something about your department's testing."

Rose takes a seat at the conference table where just about six weeks earlier they had discussed her employment duties and the testing schedules. "What's up?" she asks. Rose is new to this blaming environment, but she's already learning not to allow herself to be intimidated.

"Your department's testing isn't good enough, that's what." Kahn pulls out the customer-site report a tech support rep had shoved at him earlier that morning. He pushes it across the table to Rose. "You've been here a little more than six weeks. Why haven't you done anything about this?"

Rose reads through the customer's call log, which tracks in excruciating detail the past two-weeks' worth of problems with this particular installation at the customer's site. "I see," she says. And she does see. She sees that this customer is in a world of hurt trying to use Able Corporation's software. She doesn't see, however, how it's just a testing problem, though she refrains from responding by blaming someone else. "How can my department help in this case?" she asks.

The Exhaustive Testing Fallacy

"Isn't it obvious?" Kahn bellows. "This customer is having these problems because your department isn't doing exhaustive testing! Your testers are lazy! I told you on Day One that you'd have some serious butt-whipping to do."

"What do you mean by 'exhaustive'?" Rose asks.

Kahn smacks the table with his fist. "What? You don't know? I thought *you* were the quality expert!"

Rose takes a deep breath to calm herself. "Oh, I know what 'exhaustive' means to me. I want to know what it means to you."

Kahn rolls his eyes in exasperation. "I mean they're not testing everything and they should be!"

By now, Rose knows better than to try to talk Kahn out of something even so ridiculous to her mind as "exhaustive testing" when he's in a blaming mood. Rose thinks for a second, frowning in dismay, *Kahn believes The Exhaustive Testing Fallacy, that it's possible to test everything!* Speaking slowly, she says, "It's never possible to test *everything*."

Rose understands that Kahn doesn't know the first thing about testing, but she now sees that he doesn't even know enough to know that he doesn't know. She is tempted to tell him that the only real kind of exhaustive testing is when the tester is too exhausted to continue, but she keeps the thought to herself, replying simply, "All right, we'll look at our tests."

The Testing–Produces–Quality Fallacy

Before Kahn can respond, Rose continues, "Now, in your voice-mail, you said something about a lost sale. What's that about?"

"We lost the MegaCorp deal." Kahn shakes his head, partly in anger, partly in disbelief. "That should have been a slam-dunk sale, but when the folks at MegaCorp did an evaluation, they found a bunch of bugs in the multi-national simulations."

"Oh?" Rose pauses slightly before continuing. "You mean like the ones we found in testing?"

"What?" Kahn snaps.

"Remember? My first week here, the testers reported problems with the multi-national simulations, but you told us to stop. You said we didn't have any customers who needed that feature, so we should focus on the important stuff."

"Look," Kahn shifts impatiently in his chair, then huffs, "you're here to make the quality better. Don't get cute with me. Do what you have to do to improve quality. This meeting is over!"

Rose stands. "Okay, I understand. I'll get to work on these things." She does not say what she will do; nor does she say what she'll work on.

Walking away from Kahn's office, Rose reflects on the absurdity of his demands. *He's specifically preventing me from improving quality by keeping me from doing anything but testing, and then only allowing testing of what he thinks should be tested. He had an indication that the feature in question was broken, and he explicitly told me not to gather any more information about it. Now he's upset that I didn't fix the problem.*

Rose decides to let this go for now. She realizes that if she pursues the point, Kahn will just entrench himself further in The Testing-Produces-Quality Fallacy. Rose determines to start by slowly eradicating Kahn's deeply ingrained fallacies about testing.

The Decomposition Fallacy

As Rose passes the test lab on her way back to her office, she hears an argument brewing and detours to see what's going on.

A developer is yelling at one of her testers. "If you want to do some useful testing, tell me what happens when you run these tests on each of the modules." Barry is shouting at Suzy as he waves a sheaf of papers at her. "I've got the test data right here. Stop testing that interface and start testing these modules."

Suzy frowns and takes half a step backwards. "Look here, Barry, I'm responsible for testing this part of the system, so I'm going to test this part of the system. Testing modules is unit testing, and that's not my job."

Barry sputters, "Not your job! Not your job! Kahn is right about you testers—you *are* a bunch of lazy ignoramuses always looking for a way out of work. Look, lady, if you test the modules and the modules make up the system, then you've done your job. Test the parts and you've tested the whole!" Out of the corner of his eye, Barry notices Rose at the door. He falls silent suddenly, aware that he's probably stepped out of line.

Before Suzy can defend her position, Rose steps into the lab where both Suzy and Barry can see her. From what she's overheard, Rose recognizes that Barry is convinced that the whole is simply the sum of its parts—The Decomposition Fallacy: Test the parts and you've tested the whole. But Rose has been bitten by that assumption often enough times to know to nip it in the bud. "Excuse me," she says, quietly. In the now-still lab, her voice carries. "May I put a word in?" Not waiting for their permission, Rose steps close to Barry and speaks in a soft voice, "Don't you think it would be a good idea for the testers to decide how to test?"

Barry reddens and then rattles his papers. "Not if they don't know what they're doing, I don't!"

"Barry," Rose says, still speaking softly, "testing the modules gives us information about the modules, not about how they work together. Suzy's right. She's supposed to test the system, not the parts of the system."

The Composition Fallacy

Suzy puts her hands on her hips and glares at Barry. "See, Barry, I'm right. Besides, testing the system will automatically test the parts."

Uh-oh, Rose thinks. *Here comes The Composition Fallacy—Suzy has the idea that if you test the system as a whole, the parts that make up the system will be tested.* Rose turns to face Suzy, again speaking quietly, "Actually, Suzy, it doesn't work that way. Yes, if a module is so broken that the system can't function, we may see a problem. But a system test won't exercise the modules the way we should in order to say we really tested them."

Suzy looks confused. "But running the system tests means touching all the modules."

"Yes, it touches them, but probably doesn't reach all parts of them," Rose explains. "Think of it this way: If all you do is touch the system interface, would you say you've tested it?"

Suzy covers her mouth with her hand before mumbling, "Oh. I see what you're saying."

Now it's Barry's turn to look confused. He addresses Rose. "Okay, suppose you're right. So what do you say we should do?"

The All-Testing-Is-Testing Fallacy

"Suzy should test the system and you test the individual modules," Rose replies. "I assume you'll be doing different types of tests."

Barry shakes his head. "They're not that different. We both execute tests through the system interface. I just have these test cases I designed to stress individual parts of each module."

"Right," says Rose. "Your test cases target specific aspects of the components. Suzy's tests target specific aspects of the interactions between the components. No matter what interface you two use for testing, you're testing different things, gathering different types of information."

"But they're not that different," Barry persists. "She could do my tests just as easily as hers."

Rose feels her patience wearing thin. "Barry, you want to find out if the modules you wrote do what you expect them to do, right?" Barry nods agreement as Rose continues, "And Suzy, you're trying to find out if the system meets the requirements we discussed in our last meeting, right?" Suzy nods. "Do you both see that you have different information you're trying to glean from your tests?"

Barry shakes his head at this. "No, I don't see. I want to know if what I wrote meets the requirements as well."

Rose agrees, "Yes, but that's different from finding out whether the code does what you intend it to do. Do you see how those are two different things?"

"No, I don't!" Barry's voice rises with tension. "All I see is we're arguing semantics about test purposes when I just want to go back to my desk so I can do my job and write code."

Rose responds, somewhat less patiently, "Both of you, please come over here." She crosses the test lab to the whiteboard on the opposite wall, picks up a marker pen, and writes three words in large letters:

REQUIREMENTS   INTENT   IMPLEMENTATION

"Barry, I think you're assuming that your intent is the same as the requirements," Rose points to the center word with the marker pen and then turns to face Barry and Suzy, "but we don't know that, do we? We don't know that our understanding of the requirements at this minute is the same as your understanding of the requirements last week when you wrote the code."

Facing the whiteboard again, Rose draws a fine, straight line to connect the words Requirements and Intent, then puts a dark slash through it. "In fact," she continues, pivoting to address them again, "we have no way of finding out if what you were thinking a week ago is what is written in the requirements document now, other than to test against the implementation. So Suzy is comparing the implementation against the requirements to see if they match."

Without waiting for a reaction, Rose turns back to the board and draws a high-arching line that stretches from the word Requirements, up over Intent, to connect to Implementation. As she cites the fallacy in the belief that "all testing is testing," from the corner of her eye, she sees Barry frown. *At least he's still listening,* Rose thinks as she turns slightly to point her marker pen in Barry's direction. "You want to compare your intent to your implementation."

Rose draws another line, this time from Intent to Implementation. "If we do both of these types of testing, we'll know if all three of these things are the same. And if they aren't, we can figure out what to do about the discrepancies. But if we assume that any two of these are equal but we don't test to confirm that they are in fact equal, we're setting ourselves up for a fall later."

Looking back at Barry and Suzy, Rose sees that they both are frowning now. She explains that closely related to The All-Testing-Is-Testing Fallacy is The Everything-Is-Equally-Easy-to-Test Fallacy, which causes people to produce optimistically incorrect estimates of testing time, and also leads to their feeling helpless, that there's nothing programmers can do to make finding bugs easier. Neither Barry nor Suzy comments upon hearing Rose's explanation.

The Any-Idiot-Can-Test Fallacy

After several long seconds, Barry breaks the silence. "Okay, fine. They're different types of testing. But I still don't see why I should have to actually do the testing. I have a list of tests I want run. The actual testing is easy. It's just a matter of banging on the keyboard. Any idiot can do it. And if anybody can, Suzy should be able to handle it." Barry sneaks a sideways peek at Suzy before softening the blow, "Just kidding, sort of."

"Ah," Rose shakes her head sadly and holds up her hand to indicate to Barry and Suzy that she wants the war over. "You think testing is easy. Let me see those tests you want us to run." Barry hands the sheaf of papers to Rose.

Rose studies the documents. She suspects that with only six weeks of experience with this product, she doesn't know everything she'd need to know to design a good set of tests, but she guesses she knows enough to find holes in a bad test suite. She's not disappointed. She looks Barry in the eye. "I can see why you think testing is easy." She hesitates for an instant and then continues, "These are very basic, comparatively simple tests. Let's sit down and think through these tests some more."

To her surprise, Barry and Suzy both sit down. Rose sees that they are grudgingly willing to learn from their collective experience in designing meaningful tests to gather useful information, but they are doing what she had hoped.

Barry is about to learn that good testing is always exploratory—with future tests strongly influenced by the results of prior tests. The process is investigative, so Barry's list of tests won't stay ahead of Suzy for long. Barry sees that he may be better off giving Suzy his ideas about the motivation behind the tests, allowing her to flesh out the actual tests in the light of up-to-the-minute information about both the product and the testing.

Summary

Learning to recognize a handful of major fallacies about testing could eliminate half the gross mistakes project managers make.

Common Mistakes

1. *Believing that blame works in the long run:* You may see short-term results from blaming, but it's more like what you get by poking a dog with a stick than it is beneficial.

2. *Believing that your first impression of a problem is always correct:* First impressions are important, but testing problems

generally require a bit more analysis—especially if you find your-self pointing the fickle finger of blame.

3. *Believing that you can test anything "exhaustively":* If you demand "exhaustive testing," what you'll generally get is testers who cheat in various ways, hide from their managers, and ulti-mately rebel.

4. *Thinking you can develop software "quick and dirty" and then test quality in:* Quick and dirty is just that. Dirty. And very hard to test, besides.

5. *Skipping unit testing as redundant because system testing will catch all the bugs:* Not only won't system testing catch all the bugs, but it will take longer and cost more—more than you save by skip-ping effective unit testing.

6. *Skipping system testing in the belief that it's redundant because unit testing will catch all the bugs:* Would you fly on an airplane's maiden flight based on the assurance that all parts were tested prior to assembly?

7. *Expecting testing to produce quality:* Quality is a product of the entire development process. Poor testing can lead to poor quality, but good testing won't lead to good quality unless all other parts of the process are in place and performed properly.

10

Testing Is More Than Banging Keys

"The pupils, at his command, took each of them hold of an iron handle, whereof there were forty fixed round the edges of the frame; and, giving them a sudden turn, the whole disposition of the words was entirely changed. He then commanded six-and-thirty of the lads to read the several lines softly, as they appeared upon the frame; and, where they found three or four words together that might make part of a sentence, they dictated to the four remaining boys who were scribes. This work was repeated three or four times, and at every turn, the engine was so contrived, that the words shifted into new places, as the square bits of wood moved upside down.

"Six hours a day the young students were employed in this labour, and the professor showed me several volumes in large folio already collected, of broken sentences, which he intended to piece together; and, out of those rich materials, to give the world a complete body of all arts and sciences. . . ."

—Jonathan Swift, English Satirist (1667–1745),
Gulliver's Travels, Chapter 21.

Like Swift's professor at the Grand Academy of Lagado, Able Corporation's developer Barry thinks that testing involves lots of random actions—believing, in essence, that testing is just a matter of banging on the keyboard. To convince Barry otherwise, Rose, Able's testing manager, directs a question from left field at Barry, making it clear through a thrust-out palm that she doesn't want Suzy, one of her own testers, to answer. "Let's start with this question: How would a creature from Mars know if someone was testing?"

"Why Mars?" asks Barry, put off by the question's seeming irrelevance.

"Because it's a well-known fact that Martians can read minds. Without the ability to read minds, nobody could know for sure whether someone is testing or not, simply by observing their behavior." Rose clears her throat, and then proceeds, "That's because the real work of testing is the mental activity that precedes and accompanies the physical activity. If you're banging keys without thinking, you're not testing. And, if you're thinking but not banging keys, you might well be testing."

Barry scratches his head. "It sounds like your definition of testing is different from mine." He looks quickly at Suzy to determine whether she is about to voice disagreement, but she says nothing.

"Maybe," replies Rose, "but I'm hoping I can convince you to expand and refine your definition. In my view, testing a system is a process of gathering information about it with the intent that the information could be used for some purpose."

"That's a little abstract for me," Barry says. "Can you give some examples?"

"Sure thing," replies Rose. "Let's start with some key banging. This is the story of my fifteen-year-old cousin, Ian."

Is banging keys to no purpose a test, or not?

"Ian spent two whole days gathering performance characteristics of his new personal computer—start-up time, launch time for his e-mail program, how long it takes to print a document from his word processor, how many browser pages he can have open at one time without crashing, and so forth. He logged all this information in a notebook, which he closed and filed away at the end of the two days." Rose pauses and then looks directly at Barry. "Now you tell me: Was he testing?"

"Sounds like it," says Barry. "But why was he doing it?"

"Well, I'm not from Mars, so I couldn't read his mind and know whether he intended ever to use this information. I asked him if he was establishing a baseline against which to measure an anticipated memory upgrade, or the next release of the operating system. He said he was not.

"Then I asked him if he was testing the process by which he would take these measurements on his mother's machine. Again, no. Next I asked if he was verifying the salesman's claims, with the intention of asking for a refund if the claims proved to be untrue. Nope.

"As far as I could tell, Ian couldn't think of any reason he was banging keys except to amuse himself. So, even though he was banging keys for two days, he wasn't really noticing anything about the results, so I would say that he probably wasn't testing. What would you answer now as to whether he was testing or not?"

"All right," agrees Barry. "I can accept the view that he wasn't testing. But if a person is *not* banging keys, then he's certainly *not* testing."

"Before you lock on to that idea, and also before I let Suzy tell us what she thinks about whether Ian was testing or not, let me tell you about a job I turned down at a large insurance company before taking the job here at Able. It paid more money, but it failed The White Glove Test."

The White Glove Test

"I asked my prospective manager whether the company used a defined testing process for its testers. 'Oh, yes,' he said. 'All one-hundred-fifty use the defined test process.'

"I then asked him what that process was, and he said, 'It's defined in our testing process manual, which is kept with the CMM library.'

"I next asked him if it was the only copy. He said yes, so I asked him to show me the library.

"In the library, I put on my white glove—actually, I use a white handkerchief because I'm not the Queen of England, so I don't wear white gloves. I wrapped the handkerchief around my index finger and dragged it along the top of the Testing Process

Manual. I came away with a quarter-inch of dust. Was I testing? Let's check the results against the definition.

"My White Glove Test gave me an estimate of how long it had been since any of the company's one-hundred-fifty testers touched the manual. Also, by getting the manager to confirm that there was only one copy of the manual, I tested the company's idea of how people use manuals. So, even though I didn't bang any keys, I performed a test, a meta-test of the testing organization. I decided I didn't want to work there."

"Wow!" says Suzy, no longer able to contain herself. "Maybe *I* should have applied The White Glove Test before I came to work here."

"It wouldn't have helped," replies Barry.

"Why not?"

"Because we don't have any documented processes for testing or anything else."

The Dog Food Test

Looking at the clock, Rose proposes that the three of them continue their conversation over lunch. Suzy suggests the burger joint on the corner, but Barry disagrees, "Let's go somewhere else. Their burgers taste like dog food."

"And how do you know that?" Suzy asks, raising a skeptical eyebrow at Barry. "Have you ever eaten dog food?"

Before Barry can think up a smart retort, Rose responds, "I hope he has. If not, he's going to start soon."

Although Barry is puzzled by Rose's remark, he decides not to ask for clarification. Instead, he suggests they go around the corner to the deli for a soup-salad-and-dessert buffet, a choice that meets with Rose's and Suzy's approval.

At the deli, the three lay claim to a small, corner table and then disperse to fill their soup bowls and choose from the salad bar. As they reconvene at their table, Rose asks, "Barry, have I won you over to my view of testing?"

Barry deliberates, first dipping a fingertip in his bowl of chili, then tasting it, then picking up the pepper mill and grinding fresh black pepper onto the chili. "Partly. But you should add something about who has to do it. I mean, you can't expect developers to test. We've got more important things to do."

"Actually," Rose replies, "developers do testing in lots of ways, or at least they should."

Suzy nods in agreement, but Barry challenges Rose's point. "What ways?"

Rose glances at her watch and then answers Barry. "Okay, fair question. First of all, when I write software, I'm constantly testing. Say I write a line of code and immediately see a typo—spotting the typo is the result of my 'testing' the code with my eyes. I correct many problems before anyone else sees my code."

"Well, of course you do that. Everybody does." Barry showers his salad with pepper, causing Suzy to stifle a sneeze. "Okay, I suppose you could call that testing, but it's kind of trivial."

"All right," continues Rose. "Here's a more striking example. I used to work at a software company that built embedded software to control brakes and steering on cars. Before the software could be released, each person who had anything to do with development of that software had to drive a car using that software around a test track at a hundred miles an hour." [9]

"Cool!" Barry's admiration is barely audible behind a mouth half full of chili. "But what does that have to do with the price of beans in China?"

"First of all, it tests the workers' confidence in their product. That's important information—not definitive of course, because some developers are naturally overconfident, while others are overly modest." Rose spears a pickle slice with her fork and waits for Barry to finish his chili. "But it's a good starting place."

"Is that kind of testing at all common?" Suzy looks up from her salad just long enough to put the question to Rose.

"Well, it's common enough to have its own name—Dog Food Testing."

Barry stares suspiciously at his empty bowl. "What does that mean?"

"It's based on a saying back where I come from: 'Before you feed it to your dog, eat your own dog food.' That may or may not be good advice for dog owners, but it's excellent advice for software developers who should test their product by using it. In spite of that, I often hear software developers claim, 'Oh, we don't use our product. We leave it to the testers to do that.'"

"Well," Barry shrugs, "we don't."

"That's true, you don't use it in the course of your regular work, but you could pretend. Or you could watch one of our customers use it."

"I can see how that might be instructive," Barry acknowledges, "but it doesn't seem an adequate test. If all we did was Dog-Food Testing, wouldn't we be making—what's it called—a sampling mistake?"

Rose smiles, pleased with the way Barry is starting to understand. "You're absolutely right. For example, software developers are not typical word-processor users. They're not even typical compiler users."

Testers need testing, too.

Suzy sips tomato soup from her spoon, then puts the still-full utensil back in the bowl, blowing air from her lips. "Too spicy," she gasps, as she picks up her fork to attack a piece of spinach in her salad. "I have another question, Rose. Remember last week when you asked me to rerun a test Charlene had already performed on the Ply.Able System? You already had results, so it wasn't for information. Does that mean it wasn't really a test?"

"That depends on what you think you were testing. It could be I was testing the Ply.Able System for consistency. Or maybe I was testing the stability of the test environment. But in this case, my intention was to test Charlene's competence because she's new to our test lab. In other words, Charlene is a system, according to my definition of testing."

Suzy toys with her soup and tries another taste, this time managing to swallow a spoonful. "It makes me uncomfortable, Rose, to know you're testing us."

"That's part of my job as test manager. Now, if I hadn't told Charlene that I had you replicating her test, I'd have risked Charlene's trust, but I did tell her. And, by the way, I hope you're testing me as your manager."

"Testing you? I wouldn't do that . . ." Suzy blushes a rosy pink and appears anxious as she waits for Rose's response.

Rose barely skips a beat. "Sure you would—or at least you should—just the way you tested your soup."

You can test without consciously realizing it.

"Tested my soup? What are you talking about?"

"You took a taste and decided it was too hot, so you ate some of your salad instead," Rose replies.

"But how does that fit our definition?"

Rose is pleased to hear Suzy say *our definition*. "Whether you were aware of it or not, you were testing, because you used the result to make a decision about risk."

"Okay, so I was testing the soup. But I certainly wasn't testing you."

"Not with sips from the spoon, but when you told me that an assignment made you uncomfortable, you were testing me. You wanted to know how I would respond, and based on that, you might change your behavior in the future based on risk."

"No, I wouldn't."

"Sure you would. If I'd snapped at you, you might not be so willing to ask me any challenging questions in the future."

A demonstration is not a test.

Suzy lowers her eyes to gaze at the remains of her spinach salad, and then shifts her glance to Barry. "At least I wasn't pounding on keys."

Barry shrugs and then gets up from the table. "Either of you want dessert?" Seeing that neither woman has any interest in taking him up on his offer, Barry walks across the dining section to the buffet and is quickly absorbed in piling desserts on a plate.

With Barry out of earshot, Rose asks, "Suzy, where were you yesterday afternoon? I came to the lab three times, but you weren't there. Were you ill?"

"I'm sorry," Suzy barely whispers. "I should have told you, but I didn't have time. I was with Randolph at the office of one of his best clients. He had me design a test suite of Barry's feature set for the client to see. It was tricky because I had to be really careful not to use any test cases that invoked known bugs. I also made sure my tests didn't trigger any of the performance problems we know about."

"I'm not too happy about that," replies Rose.

"I'm sorry. Next time, I'll be sure to tell you before I leave."

"Oh, leaving is all right, if it helps Randolph—though I would like to know where you are, in case something comes up. What I'm not happy about is that you think you were doing a test when you weren't."

"But I was. I ran about twenty different test cases."

"Well, think back to our definition. According to that, you weren't testing. You were helping Randolph make an off-line sales pitch, a demonstration disguised as a test. You weren't gathering information, because you already knew exactly what Barry's program would do on all twenty cases. In fact, the job Randolph gave you was to make sure that there was no information obtained from this pseudo-test. Randolph might have been testing your technical sales ability, and you might have passed with shining colors, but you weren't testing—except for testing the gullibility of the customer."

Rose finishes her speech just as Barry sets the dessert-laden plate on their table. Still standing, Barry points at the four desserts. "Are you sure you don't want any?"

"Yum-my. I'll take a taste of the lemon fluff." Rose picks up her spoon. "Just a taste."

Suzy claps her hands together and laughs. "A sample, right? A test."

Summary

To qualify as a test, an action has to seek information that will influence action, whether or not it involves banging on keys.

Common Mistakes

1. *Thinking a computer can read minds:* Computers do what you tell them to do, whether or not that's what you really had in mind.

2. *Failing to verify software sales claims:* Banging keys doesn't do this job, though it might help if you experience frequent crashes from key-banging. Better to have a plan based on specific claims.

3. *Failing to use coverage tools (for example, The White Glove Test) in your testing:* You can build or install tools that tell you which parts of a system have never been touched by any of your tests. They may not have gathered dust, but if they haven't been touched by any test, they certainly cannot be considered tested.

4. *Thinking that coverage tests prove something is tested:* Just because you can show that all parts of the code have been touched by some test or other, you can't say that those parts have been thoroughly tested. Nor can code coverage tell you that all *functions* have been thoroughly tested. For that to be true, the tests have to be analyzed for relevance and comprehensiveness. *Thinking*, in other words.

5. *Confusing process documents with processes:* A *process* is what you actually do. A *process document* describes what someone would *like* you to do, ideally. They rarely coincide exactly, and sometimes don't overlap at all. Most processes aren't documented at all, which generally is a good thing; otherwise, we would be crushed by the weight of endless documents. It is better to spend your valuable time observing processes—what people actually do. You can use the time you save to decide which few processes would be best backed up by precise documents.

6. *Confusing documents with facts:* The previous point is a general case for such special cases as confusing test scripts with tests, confusing test reports with tests, and confusing requirements documents with requirements.

7. *Failing to "eat your own dog food":* If you are afraid of or disdainful about your product, why should anyone buy it?

8. *Using only non-representative "dogs" in a Dog Food Test:* Unless you're developing software development tools, samples composed entirely of software developers are unlikely to represent your population of users.

9. *Failing to test your testers, or testing them too much:* Everyone's job needs to be evaluated, but not incessantly. At some point, you have to trust people to do their jobs without a boss standing over them.

10. *Pretending demonstrations are tests:* You can be on the sending or receiving end of this one. I'm not sure which is worse—fooling others or fooling yourself.

11

Information Intake

*"A loud voice cannot compete with a
clear voice, even if it's a whisper."*

—Barry Neil Kaufman, *Out-Smarting Your Karma:
And Other Preordained Conditions*
(Sheffield, Mass.: Epic Century, 1996).

In William Perry and Randall Rice's useful book *Surviving the Top Ten Challenges of Software Testing,* the following four challenges pertain to pure communication problems: "Building Relationships with Developers," "Explaining Testing to Managers," "Communicating with Customers—and Users," and "Having to Say No." The other six challenges also have strong communication components, which is not surprising when you remember that testing is an information-gathering activity. [10]

Use the Satir Interaction Model to unravel communications.

In my consulting with testers and their managers, I often employ a useful model of communication adapted from the late family therapist Virginia Satir's Interaction Model. Satir is considered to be the founder of the "communication school" of family therapy and her Interaction Model tells us some surprising things about what goes on inside people's heads, including during interactions between people. Satir used this model to help people understand the complex dynamics of families as systems in which fast, mysterious interactions happen every day. I find it useful for helping software testers improve their systems of observing and communicating about software status (where fast, mysterious interactions may happen at any minute).

The full Satir Interaction Model was designed to account for what happens when people interact. I use the model to improve how I receive and give information about testing, such as when I am doing activities like the following:

- observing the behavior of systems under test
- interacting directly with others
- writing and understanding testing reports
- watching users at work, as in usability testing or beta testing
- presenting observations and conclusions
- observing myself at work, in order to improve

A model's job is to simplify a complex process, so, as a first approximation, the Satir Interaction Model breaks down any communication process into four major parts: *intake, meaning, significance,* and *response,* as shown in the following figure:

➤ intake ➤ meaning ➤ significance ➤ response ➤

Intake

During the *intake* part of the process, a person takes information from the world. Some people believe that this activity describes the entire observation process, but there is much more going on. Intake does not "just happen"; it also involves a selection process. Whether or not we recognize that we are being selective as we observe, we are actually exercising a great many choices about what we see and hear. It's in*take,* not simply in*put.*

Meaning

During the *meaning* part of the process, someone considers the sensory intake and gives it a meaning. Some people believe that the meaning lies in the data, but the same intake can have many different meanings. When a diner says to a waiter, "The soup's okay," she could mean simply that the soup is completely satisfactory, or that she'll take the soup even if it's not what she wanted, or that the soup is superb and way beyond expectations, or she could mean "stop asking about the soup and leave me alone to enjoy my meal."

In other words, intake data have no meaning until some person gives them meaning. The meaning process also interacts with the intake process. For example, certain inferred meanings may lead us to take in more information or different information. If the soup isn't exactly what the diner wants, a waiter might ask how it could be improved. But other interpretations might lead the waiter to shut off intake altogether—as with "stop asking about the soup and leave me alone to enjoy my meal."

We look at the meaning part of the process in greater detail in Chapter 12.

Significance

Data may suggest certain meanings, but never their *significance*. Is this information important to me? How important? Only the receiver can make this determination.

Why is there a signficance step? The world we perceive would be an overwhelming flood of data if we did not categorize and select information in the context of its significance. Once we have determined significance, we can give priority to a few patterns of intake and their meanings and largely ignore the rest.

The significance we assign to an intake and its meaning may lead us to alter our intake and meaning processes. For instance, if we decide that the intake is extremely important, we may stop paying attention to other sources of intake and focus our attention on just this one. Conversely, if we think the intake is unimportant, we may shift our attention away.

We examine significance in Chapter 13.

Response

During the *response* part of the process, a person formulates an action to take. Software testers and their managers are observers, but they are never *passive* observers. They may not (and should not) respond immediately to everything and anything they observe, but they do (and should) sift through and assign priorities to observations according to how important they are to the observer, and store them away to guide future actions. Testers are not interested in observation without reference to possible action. For instance, testers are especially interested in the response, "Seek more data!" We look further at response in Chapter 14.

If you're a tester trying to communicate with a manager, or a manager struggling to understand what a tester is trying to tell you, the Satir Interaction Model can help you debug your interaction.

People listen selectively.

One way communications involving testers go awry is through a failure in the intake step. Some messages are hard to take in accurately because people don't want to hear them. Managers, for example, are particularly good at selective listening about release and ship dates. A tester may say, "At the current rate we're finding and fixing bugs, there's very little chance that we can ship by the first of September." The project manager whose job is on the line is likely to hear, "Blah blah blah blah we can ship by the first of September."

How can you avoid this problem? First off, only give and accept dates in written form. Second, don't give or accept "point dates"—dates that specify a precise 24-hour period, such as "the first of September." Then, give and accept estimated dates only when they are written as ranges—"we estimate that we will release Version 4 in the August 1st to August 21st timeframe," for example—but even then, the later date will often be dropped out of the intake, with people making a mental note of only the earlier date. To emphasize the range, give estimated dates as graphs of probability versus date. I call these what's-the-chance graphs.

The source of the data influences intake.

People tend to make different responses to information received from different sources—often predetermining the importance of a message based on the sender. If you're having trouble getting people to pay attention to your test reports, try sending them via someone whose reputation will make the recipients change or drop their intake filters.

As a consultant, I often act in this intermediary role. Managers who won't listen to their own employees often listen to me. If they didn't intend to listen to me, they would be foolish to hire me in the first place.

If you discover that others are more willing to accept information you have to convey when another person delivers it, think of the knowledge as a test result. Continue testing by asking yourself, "What have I done in the past that would make people think I'm not a reliable source? What do I need to do in the future to raise their trust in me as a source?"

Examine yourself first, but in the end, you may find that the problem lies with the person with whom you are trying to communicate. Some people just won't listen to anything that comes from testers, regardless. If that's true, you're better off looking for someplace else to work, rather than try to fix your communication style—though you may need to do that, too.

Timing makes a difference.

People miss information when they're paying attention somewhere else. If you don't have someone's attention, there's no point in your providing information because that person won't be likely to accept it. For instance, developers who feel they have staked their next raise on their product passing all tests are not likely to hear a message about test failures.

In a blaming environment, managers tend to believe that constantly raising the stakes (whether monetary, emotional, or otherwise) will improve testing. But, if the stakes are too high, people will hear nothing but the blame, made deaf by the fear it engenders. For example, managers who believe their jobs are at stake if they don't ship a product on time will not be open to information that seems to increase the probability of lateness. In the extreme case—which I see rather frequently—the manager simply ignores the test reports altogether.

People can be overloaded with information.

At times, people turn off their intake, or turn it way down, when bombarded with too much information. Testers may report so many bugs that triage meetings take hours. They may write so many reports that no one can read them all. In some cases, the testers themselves may be the victims—receiving so many pages of specs that they can't possibly read them thoroughly before having to test against them.

That information overload has occurred is information in and of itself—yielding meta-information about an organization and the ways it produces and handles information. Testers who notice overload may want to modify these habits. For example, one of my clients regularly held triage meetings that tied up large numbers of key people for long periods of time. As a result, many bug reports were not triaged, or were triaged far too carelessly or too late to be helpful. We modified the triage procedure to follow three rules:

1. *Use four bug-report categories only: level 0, level 1, level 2, and level 3.* (We reduced the number of categories from ten to four.)
2. *Spend no more than one minute on any one bug report before setting it aside with a temporary "level-0" classification.* (We used a kitchen timer to enforce both this rule and Rule 3.)
3. *If time permits reexamination of temporary "level-0" bug reports, spend no more than five minutes on any one before sending it elsewhere for additional information.*

We assigned each bug report to one of four levels according to the following rationale: A *level-0* issue is blocking other testing. Something that we set aside because it couldn't be classified in one minute was deemed to be blocking testing, which, of course, it would if it led to long arguments that tied up many testers. If there was time left after we considered all bugs, we could spend another five minutes on each of the temporary level-0 bug reports. A *level 1* indicated that the product could not ship if this issue was not resolved. A *level 2* meant that the value of the product would be significantly reduced if this issue was not resolved. A *level 3* indicated a bug that would be important only if there were large numbers of similar issues when the product shipped.

Using the three rules, the triage team was able to classify the entire backlog of 129 unclassified bugs in less than two hours— sending only three bugs back for more information. The speed with which other test departments can classify and resolve bugs may vary, but long triage arguments may be telling you more about the psychology of your team than about the difficulty of classifying bugs.

You may convey more information by reducing the number of tests.

It may seem paradoxical to those who subscribe to The Test Everything Fallacy, but by reducing the amount of data generated by tests, you may actually gain more information. Here's where *significance* feeds back into the *intake* decision. Narrow your set of potential tests by asking, "Which tests will have the greatest impact on further testing and development?"

By learning the answer to this question, you can often determine what information you should find first. For instance, if a system fails to return any results when just one user is logged in, it would be silly for testers to spend weeks attempting to run performance tests based on system load.

Paradoxically, some information might seem critical but is actually irrelevant. You might think testing would be blocked if the installation fails, but installation script is often independent of the actual software. If by hook or by crook (but not by the ultimate installation script) you can get all the pieces and parts where they belong, you may be able to test the features of the software, while allowing a parallel effort to test and repair the installation script.

Seek intake from outside the box.

While cruising the Internet some years back, I read a story about a woman who called a help desk about a problem with her printer. The tech support rep asked her whether she was "running it under Windows."

"No," the woman said, "my desk is next to the door. But that's a good point. The man sitting in the cubicle next to me is under a window, and his is working fine."

True or not, this story has a grain of truth in it. Sometimes potential data lying outside our scope of attention can influence a program's behavior. Sunlight on a device can raise the temperature and cause the device to behave erratically. So too can static electricity, vibration, radar, and who knows what else? When a test machine doesn't work the way you expect, maybe somebody else used it and changed its state. Maybe the operating system has been jiggered.

Don't confuse interpretation with intake.

The human mind craves meaning. If you feed people a random bit of data, they'll struggle to divine meaning from it—and they'll move from the intake phase to the meaning phase so fast they won't be aware of doing so. Some statements that appear to convey straightforward facts are actually subject to interpretation by the receiver.

Following are a few examples I've gleaned from clients' test reports:

- *"There were too many bugs."* "Too many" for what? Maybe there were just the right number. Sometimes one is too many, and other times one hundred is okay.
- *"There were a lot of bugs."* "A lot" compared with what?
- *"There were only four bugs."* Is "only four" better or worse than expected?
- *"There were four bugs."* "There were" is an interpretation. The speaker doesn't know how many bugs "there were," only how many were found. Say, "We found four bugs," and say under what conditions they were found.
- *"Tests show that the project has to slip."* This is actually a jump ahead to the significance step. Tests themselves don't show any such thing, but someone has decided that there's only one meaning to the tests, and only one significance to that meaning.

Ask The Data Question to filter out interpretations.

When someone presents you with test interpretations when you want data, use The Data Question: *What did you see or hear (or smell or taste or feel) that led you to that interpretation?* Generally, you will have to keep repeating The Data Question until you reach the level of meaning-free data you desire. Then, when you finally have the purified data, you can reverse the process and proceed to making meaning of a statement such as "we found four bugs."

Summary

Intake is an active process. Try to be aware of factors that limit your intake, sources of information, and how data may be flavored by biased meaning. You are not a victim, having data *put* into you, but are at least potentially in control of what you *take in*.

Common Mistakes

1. *Not thinking about what information you're after:* Don't just take what comes. You have choices.
2. *Not actively seeking the information you're after:* Ninety-nine percent of information is useless for the task of testing, but there's still plenty if you know how to sift the gold from the dross.
3. *Conflating intake and meaning:* Data are meaningless until someone determines their meaning. Different people give different meanings to the same data. Gather data, then sit down and ponder at least three possible meanings.
4. *Forbidding testers to look for bugs in certain places:* Those forbidden places can be lush with data to intake.
5. *Failing to provide adequate equipment and tools for testing:* Would you expect a pathologist to work without a microscope? What is a tester but a software pathologist? (Please note that tools need not be commercial packages—as elaborated in a later chapter.)
6. *Succumbing to The Golden Elephant Syndrome:* Software test expert James Bach calls one of the terrible pathologies of modern testing The Golden Elephant Syndrome: A white elephant may be a big, useless thing, but if it's made of gold and costs a lot of

money, it's tempting to some people to try to use it anyway. Expensive test tools can cause a lot of trouble if they are badly designed, unreliable, or force testers to test in ways they wouldn't have chosen except that it's convenient for the tool. If such a tool were cheap, we wouldn't hesitate to throw it away. But if it's expensive, the person who bought it doesn't want to look like a fool—and thus becomes a bigger fool.

12

Making Meaning

"INDECISION, n. The chief element of success; 'for whereas,' saith Sir Thomas Brewbold, 'there is but one way to do nothing and diverse ways to do something, whereof, to a surety, only one is the right way, it followeth that he who from indecision standeth still hath not so many chances of going astray as he who pusheth forwards'—a most clear and satisfactory exposition on the matter."

—Ambrose Bierce, American Author (1842–1914),
The Unabridged Devil's Dictionary,
eds. D.E. Schultz and S.T. Joshi
(Athens, Ga.: University of Georgia Press, 2002).

Despite the fictitious Sir Thomas Brewbold's gobbledygook pronouncement, indecision, when applied in the interpretation of test data, is indeed a fine thing—up to a point. That point is defined by The Rule of Three, which says, in this context of test-data interpretation: *If you can't think of at least three possible interpretations of the test result, you haven't thought enough.*

Let's look at some examples, all starting with Rocky, a tester who gives the following bad news: "Tests show that the project has to slip. There were four bugs." After filtering out Rocky's interpretations, you're left with "There were four bugs." Ginger is the project manager. What does she do now?

Case 1: Four Bugs—Five Meanings

Ginger asks Rocky, "What did you test?"

"I tested X-TERMINATOR, the whole thing," Rocky replies indignantly.

Ginger has her suspicions, but she tries to sound noncommittal. "Oh, good. I'd like to read the bug reports."

Rocky's tone is now defensive. "I haven't written them down yet."

Ginger thinks, *If it's not written down and you haven't even told anyone, is it a test result?* but she merely asks, "Oh? Why haven't you?"

Rocky looks at her, the expression on his face clearly showing that he thinks she's incredibly stupid. "It should be obvious. X-TERMINATOR is the bug-tracking system, and one of the bugs is that I can't log in to report bugs."

"Oh," says Ginger, puzzled and thinking aloud. "In that case, I wonder what the other three bugs can be?"

"There are three spelling errors on the log-in screen."

Ginger might come away from this brief exchange with any or all of the following five meanings:

(a) Ginger might conclude that Rocky's statement that he tested "the whole thing" isn't a very useful characterization of what was tested, because if Rocky couldn't log on, what could he have tested?

(b) Ginger might wonder whether the problem with log-in could be just a glitch in the log-in, which possibly could be fixed in a few minutes. She doesn't know very much about the state of X-TERMINATOR, but it occurs to her that if her developers can't even get the log-in right, maybe the rest of the system is even worse.

(c) Ginger has some issues with the way Rocky has reported the situation, as well as with Rocky's initiative. She might speculate that although he may not have been able to log onto X-TERMINATOR, he could still have accessed whatever reporting system the testers were using before or by using good old-fashioned paper and pencil. She might also wonder why the testers are using an untested bug-reporting system anyway.

(d) Ginger might wonder whether the purpose of Rocky's testing is simply to check out a demo copy of a bug-tracking database. If that is the case, she supposes that the log-on problem may be a trivial installation difficulty.

(e) Ginger knows that X-TERMINATOR is supposed to be a commercial product, but thinks that with three spelling errors found on the log-in page, X-TERMINATOR might not be a commercial-quality product.

Case 2: Four Bugs—Seven Meanings

In an alternate universe, the case starts with the same intake, but runs a different course. Ginger asks Rocky, "What did you test?"

"I tested X-TERMINATOR, the whole thing," Rocky replies indignantly.

Ginger has her suspicions, but she tries to sound noncommittal. "Oh, good. I'd like to read the bug reports."

Rocky hands her a one-page printout. "Here they are."

Ginger reads the bug reports and finds the following:

Bug 1: Account #1 has the wrong read/write permission.
Bug 2: Account #2 has the wrong read/write permission.
Bug 3: Account #3 has the wrong read/write permission.
Bug 4: Account #4 has the wrong read/write permission.

Let's break from the story again and examine some of the meanings Ginger might form from the bug reports.

(a) "The whole thing" isn't a very useful characterization of what was tested.

(b) Rocky did most of his testing in the permissions area.

(c) Most of the bugs in X-TERMINATOR are in the permissions area.

(d) Maybe there's only one underlying fault related to the four reports.

(e) Rocky may not be very bright because he's not even suggesting that there might be a relationship among these bugs.

(f) Rocky may be very bright because he doesn't automatically assume that there's only one bug and throw away supposedly redundant data.

(g) Rocky hasn't said what constitutes wrongness, nor has he explained by what principle or mechanism he makes that determination. Each one of these reports could refer to a different set of wrong read/write permissions.

Notice that Case 1 and Case 2 begin in exactly the same way, with exactly the same report being handed to the project manager. Evidently, there's more to test reports than simply writing them.

Case 3: Four Bugs—Make Your Own Meanings

Want to test yourself to determine whether you really understand The Rule of Three? Yes? Good. Test yourself by writing your own case that begins the same way as Case 1 and Case 2, with "There are four bugs," but based on your own experience.

James Bach sent me the following case in response to my invitation to testers to test themselves starting at Ginger's comment, "Oh, good. I'd like to read the bug reports."

> "I can just tell you," says Rocky. "Bug number one is that this product appears to be based on pirated source code from a bug-tracking system I wrote and released as shareware. Bug number two is that the documentation appears to be a plagiarized version of the manual from my bug-tracking system. Bug number three is that the product is supposed to be called 'X-TERMINATOR,' yet, as you can see, the splash screen clearly says 'ROCKY'S BUG MANAGER.' The fourth bug is that my copyright notice has been removed! If you need to see a written report, I can have my lawyer send you a certified copy."

What am I trying to show by these examples? One goal is to show you that *interpreting data to make meaning* requires diligence and an open mind. Certainly you should see that a simple bug count is less than useless as a test report unless you use it as a starting point for further investigation. Don't make the mistake of thinking that fancier reports are any better. If you think you have a reporting system that doesn't seem to require reading and analyzing and interpreting to assign meaning, all that means is that you're being manipulated by your reporting system. No matter how test results are presented to you, be aware that you can be misled by their seeming objectivity. Notice that The Rule of Three says to search for *at least three meanings.* You're welcome to go for more than three, as long as you check them all out.

Know what you're expecting before you interpret.

Computer scientist Alan Perlis once told me, "There are no wrong programs, only different programs." I didn't understand him until a few months later when the team I was working with ran into a difficult problem. I was designing an experiential training program for computer operators, and wanted a simulation that would allow operators to practice restarting the operating system after it crashed while running several programs simultaneously. It's not something you can really learn in a lecture, so I needed a program that would crash the operating system in random ways, at random times.

Running this crash-simulator over and over would give the operators plenty of practice—but try as we might, we couldn't design a program that crashed the operating system in this way. We were about to give up in frustration when one member of the team said, "Wait a minute. We don't have to *build* a random-crash simulator. We already have one."

And, indeed, we did, and it was infamous. Some physicists had been trying for years to simulate a certain atom with a huge, out-of-control FORTRAN program. Each of us had, at various times, been called in to help them fix this program, which crashed at random times and brought down the operating system. We took a copy, froze it, and trained our operators with it.

For the next four years (maybe longer but that's when I left the scene), the physicists never got their program "correct." For us, though, it worked from the moment we started using it. It never had any bugs, and never had to be changed. What was a failure for the physicists' purposes was a perfect program for us. It's not often you find a perfect program.

This funny (or tragic) case shows that if you don't know what a program is supposed to do, you can never say with certainty that it's wrong. You have to know what you're expecting before you give meaning to a test report, otherwise everything looks or sounds right. That's why I'm a strong advocate of the test-first philosophy, whereby developers write their tests to include

107

expected results before they write a line of code. It's what we did fifty years ago, but the practice was gradually lost when industry trends separated testing from development.

That separation occurred initially because it's psychologically difficult for people to test their own programs. There's still significant risk if you rely on test-first without pair programming or some other process that casts more than one pair of eyes, and more than one brain, on a program. Sometimes, test-first enthusiasts think they don't also need independent testers. Since their own testing is mainly at the unit level, followed by acceptance testing that is primarily confirmatory, they may be right to go without independent testers if the programs are simple and stand-alone. Working at higher levels of integration with higher levels of required safety, they'd be well advised to use additional tests performed by specialized professionals.

What if you don't know what's expected?

If you don't know what a product is expected to do when interpreting test results, you can start by asking the following questions:

- *Does this thing do what the people who count want it to do?*
- *Does it not do what the people who count don't want it to do?*
- *What do these test results tell me about that?*

But what if it's not clear what the people who count want? In that case, you can report what you thought they wanted, what you found, and list the discrepancies. If it's helpful to do so, you might want to suggest some interpretations of what they could want, and perhaps how you developed those ideas. But be careful you don't over-influence them with your ideas. If you do, they may seem to agree, only to say when you're finished testing, "No, that's not what I wanted."

For example, suppose a test shows that a dialogue box was one pixel to the left of what was specified. Is this okay, or not?

It depends.

We can construct situations in which it would matter very much and situations in which it wouldn't matter at all. So, you can deal with this ambiguity by not making any meaning. Simply report: "The dialogue box is one pixel to the left of what was specified. Is this acceptable?"

Use the information you have.

Generally, you can't make meaning of a test report without considering information that's not in the report. At least start with the information you already have before you blindly ask for more. Similarly, take care to make the best use of the information you already have.

Consider the following example: Doug, a manager, is poring over bug reports, test reports, specifications, and requirements documents. He is up to his eyeballs in paper. One of his employees, Helen, asks, "Doug, what are you doing?"

Doug replies, "I have a feeling that something isn't quite right with the system. I don't think we're going to make our ship date. I want evidence, so I'm reviewing all the information we have to date."

Helen scratches her head and looks puzzled. "Doug, what happened in the acceptance test that Operations was supposed to run last week?"

Doug looks up and sighs, "We don't have any results from that test, so I can't use it."

"Why don't we?"

"Because they couldn't get the software installed."

"Then what more information do you need?"

That Operations was not able to install the software is itself a crucial test result.

Use indirect information.

When properly documented, bug reports contain much more information than just the location of a bug and how to replicate the problem. Pay attention to the extra information that testers sometimes consider to be bureaucratic overhead: the date and time each test was run; the date and time each report was submitted; who ran each test; who submitted each report; unambiguous identification of the software and version(s) tested, the operating system(s), the browser(s), the computer(s), the configuration(s), the test tool(s), and the source language(s); references to earlier bug reports; and all sorts of free-form comments. Organize the collection and entry of this data to be as easy and as automatic as possible, or human beings won't tolerate it.

Many of the most difficult bugs can be understood only in terms of these seemingly incidental data. For example, the bug report history may tell you that reports of a particular bug have been circulating without being resolved. You may garner strong clues to the meaning of certain bugs that appear and disappear by noticing version changes in the testing infrastructure. Keep your eyes and mind open.

Use the information you don't have.

A story circulating on the Internet points out the importance of knowing how to infer meaning based on information that is missing. I've changed the names to disguise anyone real who might be implicated, but the story goes as follows: Jarrod is testing the dial-up function of an online system that's primarily used via a high-speed connection. He reports to Rosella, "I installed the software okay, and it dialed fine. I could hear that. Then I could hear the two computers connecting, but then the connection failed."

Rosella knows that "the connection failed" is an interpretation, so she uses The Data Question to dig out more information: "What did you see or hear that led you to believe that the connection failed?"

"The sound all stopped."

"The sound might have stopped for a lot of reasons. What led you to believe the connection had failed?"

"I wasn't sure what the silence meant, so I picked up the phone to see if they were still connected."

"And what did you see or hear?"

"I didn't hear anything, but on the screen, I saw the message, NO CARRIER. So I knew the connection had failed."

The missing information here was that Jarrod doesn't have much experience with dial-up connections. Consequently, Rosella assigned him to work alongside someone who had that experience.

The same word may have several different meanings.

Rosella knew that the word "failed" could have multiple meanings, and the incident reminded her of an Internet riddle:

Q: "How do you know if you're from California?"

A: "You know you're from California when your wife says 'pick up Granola on the way home,' and you go to the day-care center."

In the other 49 states, granola is a breakfast cereal, but Californians name their kids Granola or Rainbow or Ecstasy, much to the confusion of those who try to make meaning of their utterances.

Another common California word is "fault"—as in San Andreas Fault. Outside of earthquake country, "fault" tends to suggest blame, not something to avoid when buying a house. But in testing parlance, when we talk about software faults, we mean underlying fissures (in the software) rather than blame. Testers are supposed to be finding fissures, not blaming people. When a tester says there's a fault, they're not imputing blame. At least, you hope they're simply finding opportunities for improvement, so check it out before people turn defensive.

"Same" may not be identical.

You might think that numbers have one and only one precise meaning. Not so. Back in 1956, when FORTRAN was invented, I had one heck of a time locating the fault behind an intermittent failure in a compiled program. It turned out that FORTRAN had a bug. The number 1.2 was not equal to 1.2 when one instance had been compiled as a source-code constant and the other had been read in as data. One person on the FORTRAN team had written the conversion routine for source-code decimal constants to floating-point binary, but a different person had written the conversion routine for decimal input constants.

Ever since, I've been suspicious when interpreting things—words, numbers, pictures, graphs, you name it—that look identical but actually come from different sources. You, too, might want to be suspicious when two things are (supposedly) the same. And so you may want to substitute the phrase "appear the same" for "the same," which will lead you to a less optimistic interpretation of what you take in.

Sometimes it's better to be imprecise.

Paradoxically, when you're trying to communicate meaning, it's sometimes more effective to use ambiguous language than to be very precise. That's because people often skip right past the opportunity to determine meaning and go straight to assigning significance. Their instant emotional reaction to an unconsciously assumed meaning then prevents them from hearing the meaning you intended. For example, you may want to use inexact words, like "bug" or "issue," if you want to be understood by people who cannot disconnect from the blame connotation of "error" or "fault."

If you want to communicate effectively in a situation in which meanings can differ, think about the receiver. Try to use the receiver's terminology and listen to the tone of any spoken response, even if you think the person is being unreasonable. Let a customer/tech-support dialogue I found circulating on the Internet be your model:

Tech Support Rep:	"All right . . . now double-click on the file-manager icon."
Customer:	"That's why I hate this software—because of the icons. I'm a Protestant. I don't believe in icons!" *(The emotional charge in the customer's voice tells the rep that the customer is not kidding.)*
Tech Support Rep:	"Well, that's just an industry term, sir. I don't believe it was meant to—" *(Here, the rep tries to be logical and reasonable in order to "correct" the customer's emotional association of the word icon with religion.)*
Customer:	"I don't care about any 'industry' terms! I don't believe in icons." *(The customer*

shows even more emotion in not letting the rep finish his sentence. "Correcting" people's emotions almost certainly guarantees that they will not receive your meaning.)

Tech Support Rep: *(The rep finally understands the customer's emotion.)* "Well, uh, why don't you click on the little picture of a filing cabinet. Is 'little picture' okay?"

Customer: *[mouse click]*

Summary

Data do not speak for themselves, nor are they unambiguous. It is up to human beings to attach meaning to data they take in, and each person does so differently. It's best to keep in mind that there are many possible interpretations of the same data.

Common Mistakes

1. *Jumping to conclusions about what data mean:* Think of at least three possible meanings before you act. (In other words, act according to The Rule of Three.)

2. *Running tests without documenting the expected results in advance:* Psychologically, it's all too tempting to declare that a test has been successful and that the product is bug-free when it "looks right." In advance of testing, record your expectations for test results, but be ready for surprises as well.

3. *Over-documenting expected results in advance:* It's easy to carry the previous point too far. Generally, you don't need to write down things like, "The computer should not explode, the operating system should not crash, the user should not be injured, errors should produce error messages, the application should load and not destroy other applications, and execution should not take so long that the user thinks the system has gone into an infinite loop." All of these statements are probably true, but distract from other, more valuable, anticipated results. Such expected results could be listed once for all tests.

4. *Trying to make meaning all by yourself:* Many minds make multiple meanings. Involve the entire team to decrease the chance of overlooking an important conclusion.

5. *Thinking that meaning completely determines significance:* It's not sufficient to apply The Rule of Three when making meaning out of intake. The same meaning can have different importance to different people. "Many minds make multiple imports" doesn't have the alliteration of the previous motto, but you will do well to remember it anyway.

13

Determining Significance

What *is* significance? *Significance* is the importance attached to the bug by the person who gets to decide what to do about that bug. At first glance, this definition seems straightforward, but let's see how it plays out in the following scenario:

Cheri works for BQ Enterprises as project manager for Bloblin Quinella (a game about betting on bloblin races). We catch up with her as she is leading her team in a strategy meeting. It's a few hours before she is to head off to San Francisco for the monthly Galactic Game Gathering. At this month's Gathering, she plans to introduce Version 3.0 of Bloblin Quinella, but her plan is seriously jolted when Marv, the test manager, announces, "We have to hold up the launch. We've just found a terrible bug. At random times, when a player is racing Bloblin the Goblin, BG disappears from one place and reappears in another."

With all eyes upon him, Marv takes a deep breath and glances furtively at Cheri's suitcase, which is stashed in the corner by the door, ready for her departure. He continues, "If the folks at the Gathering see this defective product, they'll laugh us out of business. Cheri, you've got to unpack and stay here so you can help us get this fixed for introduction at next month's Gathering."

It is clear to everyone on the team that Marv attributes great significance to this bug.

Rulon, the marketing manager, waves Marv's concerns aside, saying, "We can't do that. A successful introduction of BQ 3.0 at this Gathering will grab us ten percent more market share than we'll get introducing it a month from now, and that's worth at least a hundred million dollars." For Rulon, this bug is trivial, at least when compared in significance to the potential $100 million in lost market share.

Everyone falls quiet. Cheri thinks, *If the bug shows up at the Gathering, I will lose my job.* Her first reaction is that the bug is very significant, but then she thinks things through a step further: *If we don't even show BQ at the Gathering, I'll lose my job.* Cheri's significance is personal, and depends on her subjective assessment of the chances of losing her job in two different ways.

Phil, the salesman who will travel with Cheri to San Francisco to lead the demo, sees that Cheri is in a quandary and tries to help out. "Don't worry, Cheri. I'll tell the audience that this disappearing act isn't a bug at all but is a feature that no other game has. It will sell a million copies." To Phil, this isn't a bug but, as a feature, it is significant in yet another way.

Up to this point, Netta, who designed and built Version 3.0, hasn't said anything, but now she stares down at her notes and speaks calmly, "Not to worry, Cheri. I can fix this bug in fifteen minutes and you can still catch your plane. If I don't fix it here, I'll have to go with you to San Francisco and I really can't be out of town this week."

"No, don't!" screeches Phil. "Don't you dare remove that feature!"

Different people attach different importance to the same information.

In this scenario, we can easily see that the significance of a bug does depend on who gets to decide what to do about that bug. Unless Cheri's boss overrides her decision, Cheri will decide. The significance of the bug to the others counts only to the extent that Cheri buys into their view. Naturally, the others think their understanding of the bug's significance is the "real" significance, but Cheri's job is to weigh all views together to come up with the overall project significance of this bug—if indeed it is a bug.

Ideally, Cheri will extract from all team members—and from an attorney in BQ Enterprises' legal department—the significance from their own point of view:

From Marv, the test manager, she wants to know, "What impact will this have on testing if we leave it, or if we fix it?"

From Rulon, the marketing manager, she needs to know, "What impact will this have on future sales if we leave it, or if we fix it?"

From Netta, the Version 3.0 designer and builder, she needs to know, "What impact will this have on development if we leave it, or if we fix it?"

From Phil, the salesman, she wants to know, "What impact will this have on quarterly revenue if we leave it, or if we fix it?"

From an attorney she'll contact by telephone, she wants to know, "What impact will this have on our liability if we leave it, or if we fix it?"

And from Swanson, who isn't present at Cheri's meeting but is important as the head of the support team, she will ask, "What impact will this have on support costs if we leave it, or if we fix it?"

With answers to these questions, and answers from any other factions that have an interest in Bloblin Quinella, Cheri can assess the significance for the entire project.

Or can she?

Public significance may differ from private.

Assessing significance would be simple if everyone were logical, fair, and open. However, people may have hidden personal agendas that diminish or intensify their answers to Cheri's questions. Consider a few of these possibilities and motives:

Marv was hoping to attend a once-in-a-lifetime, rare-base-ball-card auction in San Francisco the weekend after the Gathering. If the demo is postponed, he'll have to pay for his own trip to California.

Rulon thinks he's next in line for a project manager job. If the demo fails, Cheri may lose her job and he'll get promoted to it.

Netta's rich uncle, Sylvester, is visiting, and he's rumored to be writing a new will. If she's out of town at the Gathering, her cousin Kirt will show Sylvester a good time, and she may lose out on a huge inheritance.

Swanson feels that tech support doesn't get enough respect. He thinks that if he can make tech support look like it can easily handle this problem, he will boost his stock with upper management.

So, if Cheri is to make a sensible estimate of significance, she will somehow have to filter out all personal agendas—including her own.

Significance depends on context.

Further complicating Cheri's ability to determine significance is that it is not just a property of a bug and a person, but also depends on the context. For instance, most people would attribute different significance to an error in a piece of code that has already posted several dozen errors than they would to the first error ever recorded in a component. Perhaps this n-th error signifies an error-prone piece of work—early bug findings are the best predictor of a component's future behavior. Lots of bugs found quickly suggests there will be lots more bugs found in the long run.

That's one reason we want to record all bugs. If we fail to record some, we may think there aren't many early bugs, and may thus misjudge the significance of our findings. The result is that we hide the fact that we're going to have trouble with this component later on.

Yet another complication: We can often merely guess at the probability that some user will actually experience the failure induced by the fault. A failure might cost thousands if experienced, but if only one user in ten billion is likely to experience it, how significant is that?

Statistically, the expected value of a fault is the probability of experiencing it times the cost if it is experienced. Some people consider the significance of something to be directly related to its expected value. If, for example, you experience a failure every time you use a certain system, and you use the system once a day, but the cost for each failure is only a penny, then the significance if equated to expected value is $3.65 a year (plus a penny more in leap years). On the other hand, if you expect to experience this failure once a year but it will destroy all your data and cost $20,000 to recover, the monetary significance is $20,000 a year.

And yet, even if you use the expected value, there's another complication: Who will incur the cost of a failure? And do we care? When my niece wrote her first book, she used a word processor to produce camera-ready copy from which the manufacturer printed books. A bug in the word processor caused a word to be omitted from the text every ten pages or so. My niece didn't notice the problem until after the first print-run, in which a thousand or more copies of the book were printed. She was devastated. It happened that the team that built the word processor was a client of mine, so I reported the bug to it.

"Oh, we know about that bug," the team leader told me.

"And you didn't fix it?"

"We decided not to. It only happens if you have a document longer than two hundred pages or so, and most users are smart enough not to put all their eggs in one basket. If we tried to fix it, we might create some other bug that would affect thousands of users."

In other words, my client didn't consider my niece's manuscript all that important, though it sure was important to her. (As mine are to me. I immediately stopped using this word processor for my manuscripts—and my client didn't really care. All the authors out there don't constitute a significant part of its market.)

You can't always judge significance in money terms.

Back at BQ Enterprises, as Cheri and her team continue debating the significance of the bug/feature, more complications arise. First comes a call-back from one of the company's lawyers, reminding them that two boys had killed themselves the preceding year trying to imitate a feature from one of BQ's competitors' game.

"What if some kid dies trying a disappearing act, in imitation of BG?" the attorney's voice booms over the speaker-phone "We'll be sued for millions."

"Whoa," shouts Netta. "You're talking about human life. You can't put a price on that."

But, of course, people do just that all the time. Permit me to digress: In the 1930s, when the Golden Gate Bridge was built, eleven workers died during construction. At the time, that was a new safety record. Bridge builders expected one fatality per million dollars in construction costs, so it was expected that thirty-five workers would die during construction. If they couldn't put a price on human life, the bridge would never have been built.

Builders of the Golden Gate Bridge also put a price on human life by deciding to suspend a safety net under the floor, which saved the lives of nineteen workers. Between 1959 and 1964, however, the builders of the Verrazano-Narrows Bridge didn't provide nets. When three fatalities provoked a job action, the builders decided lives were more significant than saving money, and so provided nets.

And, about one hundred years earlier, when the Brooklyn Bridge was being built, twenty or thirty workers died—but nobody knows for sure because worker deaths weren't significant enough to bother keeping good or permanent records.

On NASA's Project Mercury governing the first U.S. man-in-orbit flights, I was part of a team that had to attach significance to human deaths. Our bug-significance numbering classification reflected our commitment to safety. The top categories were these:

- Level 0:   Someone could die as a result of this software fault.
- Level 1:   A mission could be aborted as a result of this fault.
- Level 2:   Launch of a mission or pickup of returning astronauts could be delayed as a result of this fault.
- Level 3:   We would incur additional costs as a result of this fault.

Level 0 always trumped everything else, and I was specifically designated by T.J. Watson, Jr., then president and chairman of IBM, to guard against the possibility of any level-0 bug slipping through. If I couldn't stop someone from overriding a level-0 bug, I was to send the person to T.J. in New York. Fourteen people tried to override, but when I said they had to take their case to Watson, they all backed down. He had the last word on significance, which apparently put their arguments in a different context.

Don't put too fine a point on it.

The value of a human life is always subjective; in fact, so are all
significance measures. Many companies perform numerological
gyrations to try to make their significance judgments seem objective. Don't be fooled—either by these folks, or into tricking yourself that significance is objective.

To counter these pseudo-objective schemes, examine the
meta-significance of a situation. Start by asking yourself, "How
good are my estimates?" I once had a client who determined bug
significance with a scale that ran from zero to one hundred.
Endless hassles went on for hour after hour in meetings to bump
significance up or down a point. I kept track of how much time the
client spent ranking bugs, then pointed out that virtually all of
them could have been repaired in the time it took to decide which
would be repaired first. After that, the number of categories was
reduced to four:

- Level 0: This issue is blocking other testing.
- Level 1: Our product cannot be used if this issue isn't
  resolved.
- Level 2: The value of our product will be significantly
  reduced if this issue isn't resolved.
- Level 3: This issue will be important only if there are
  large numbers of similar issues when the
  product is shipped.

These four categories provide an adequate level of detail for testers
to use when determining significance from the testing point of
view—one of several perspectives that the deciding executive will
want to consider.

Address significant problems first.

Although the testers' ideas of significance shouldn't determine
what is done about a found failure, they should influence the order
in which various tests are executed. If test-first is a good idea, then
significance-first is even better. Why? You might perform an infinite number of tests, but if you actually perform even an enormous

number of tests, you would likely lose the valuable information among all the worthless crud. The number of tests performed should be as small as possible, but no smaller. You can't choose them perfectly, of course, but you can choose quite well if you estimate the significance of each test, then perform the most significant tests first. If your estimates are any good, then, whenever you decide to stop testing, you will have done the best you could within the time you had.

Listen to your emotional reactions.

One curious thing about computer programs is that they can sometimes be right for the wrong reasons. An oft-cited example is software designed to calculate leap-year dates correctly. Leap years, as everyone over the age of ten surely knows, come every four years, in years divisible by four—2012, 2016, 2020, and so forth.

What not everybody knows is that three out of every four turn-of-the-century years—1500, 1900, 2100, 2200, and so on—are not leap years. Except that every 400 years, a leap year does occur—1600, 2000, 2400, and so forth. Got that?

One of the subscribers to my online forum SHAPE (Software as a Human Activity Practiced Effectively) understood the exception and conducted some tests using the leap-year algorithm in a popular spreadsheet program. What David found was that the day after February 28, 1900, was identified as February 29, 1900, even though 1900 was not a leap year. Apparently, the spreadsheet developers oversimplified their leap-year calculation.

From that result, I guessed that 2100 would also be identified as a leap year in this spreadsheet, but David said no. "The spreadsheet got 2100 right (not a leap year). I don't know how you could code it to get an error for 1900 and no error for 2100. Maybe they put in a special-case check? <shudder>" That online shudder expressed David's emotional reaction, and mine, too.

That's what significance is—the emotional impact of the meaning you attach to the test result. For instance, if I determine that a bug in some software I bought makes it unusable, I might say, "Oh, that's okay. I can afford ninety-nine dollars, so it's not worth fussing about it." But if I were flat broke, I might attach a different significance: "That's *completely* unacceptable. I'm going to Small Claims Court to sue to get my money back!" Alternatively, the significance I attach to the bug might not have to do with money at all, but instead might be attached to a bias I have against or in favor of the software vendor.

As an individual user of this popular spreadsheet, I might not be bothered by this leap-year bug because I wasn't around in 1900, and won't be in 2100. But if I were hoping to incorporate this spreadsheet in software I design and sell to financial institutions that write hundred-year loans and leases, this bug might cost me a lot of business.

I might be very worried (a significant emotion) by the difference between the particular spreadsheet's handling of 1900 and 2100 because my model of what's going on inside the black box has just collapsed. If I had been the project manager, I hope I would have asked my tester to follow up with some additional tests, and so that's just what I asked David to do.

He responded: "Hmm. Well, I'm not sure if this is what you're looking for, but I modeled a test in the spreadsheet by creating seven columns, listing days Sunday through Saturday. I began with the date 1/1/1900. According to the spreadsheet, New Year's Day in 1900 was a Sunday. It was also the first calendar day the spreadsheet supports. I stepped forward through each successive day to see how the calendar works out. Sure enough, it showed that 1900 was a leap year with February 29 landing on a Wednesday."

David then compared the days of the week with the answer at http://www.earth.com/calendar. He discovered that the first of January in the year 1900 was actually a Monday, not a Sunday. Corroboration of this can be found at http://www.timeanddate .com/calendar/?country=1&year=1900. So, the explanation for how there could be an error for 1900 and no error for 2100 was that the spreadsheet has two bugs that cancel each other out:

1. It starts on a Sunday when 1/1/1900 was a Monday.
2. It adds 2/29/1900 when 1900 was not a leap year.

The result is that January 1900 and February 1900 are completely messed up, but the days of the week line up correctly from 3/1/1900 forward. What's the significance of all this? For me, were I the project manager, the significance is in understanding what the developers were doing "under the covers." It could well be a special case (yuck), or it could be that they had a table of dates including days of the week and did not generate the calendar on the fly at all. But the important thing to note is that I don't have a clue as to what they were doing. And that's significant enough.

This spreadsheet story tells a tale similar to one that Joel Spolsky reported on his Joel-On-Software blog, but the difference is that Joel was actually on the development team for the spreadsheet and dealt with the issues personally. For his account, see http://www.joelonsoftware.com.

Summary

Our emotions carry information about how important things are. If we pay attention to emotions, listen, and address important matters before unimportant matters, we'll be doing the best we can with the data we have.

Common Mistakes

1. *Confusing repair difficulty with significance:* Some classification schemes are based on code analysis, but fixing a bug is only one of its potential costs. Don't confuse the type of bug with the significance of the bug. A system crash could be insignificant, and a typing error could be disastrous. In one case I know, a mistyped phone number that appeared on one company's monthly invoices cost at least one person his life when the ambulance service whose phone number was mistakenly printed on the invoices was swamped with erroneous calls.

2. *Misjudging the significance of the speed of a response:* If test results or the solution to a problem become available more quickly than we anticipate they should, we "suspect" that they can't be correct. Likewise, if the time it takes to generate an answer matches our expectations, we "know" it's been carefully and correctly worked out.

Suppose, for example, that operators on Earth ask the computers on the Mars Orbiter to perform a calculation, and they receive an answer in less than five minutes. They undoubtedly would think something deeply wrong (such speed would be made virtually impossible by the time delay of transmitting the request to Orbiter's computers). If they receive the answer in twenty minutes, they cannot necessarily assume that everything is correct, but the time-for-transmittal information does have significance.

3. *Failing to realize that significance is political:* For example, going to jail is not measurable solely in monetary terms.

4. *Believing there is a "rational" or objective way to assess significance:* You may use numbers and algorithms to assist you, but the final assessment step is always to measure your emotional reactions to those numbers.

5. *Failing to reassess significance as new information becomes available:* Significance is a property of an entire system, including the system or process that built that system. Review your assessments on a regular basis, and be prepared to change.

6. *Allowing lullaby language to influence your assessment of significance:* Certain words shade information with meaning, whether we use them consciously or unconsciously. When someone says, "The response *should* be *very fast*," what does that mean, exactly? What meanings do "should," "very," and "fast" give to the stated information? [11]

7. *Ignoring the significance of your actions on the project team itself:* Testers are often so emotionally attached to *testing* that they are disappointed to know that bugs they find will not be fixed in the next release. They might be de-motivated, thinking on the next round of testing, *These people will not fix this bug so why should I report it?* Nobody likes to have their work ignored. Try to distinguish between ignoring and consciously choosing not to fix some bugs.

14

Making a Response

"Being deeply learned and skilled, being well trained and using well spoken words; this is good luck."
—Buddha (Siddhartha Gautama), Indian Philosopher and
Founder of Buddhism (ca 563 B.C.–ca 483 B.C.).
For this and other wise expressions, see
http://www.buddhanet.net/e-learning/qanda09.html.

The right response to bugs should be simple:

Find 'em; figure 'em; fix 'em.

Early in a project, we do this FFF, but as the tide of bugs grows, our luck runs out and we don't have enough time to make the right response. Why does this happen, and how should we respond?

Is it bad luck or bad management?

Some years ago at IBM, several of us did a study of a dozen failed projects, looking for commonalities. Our main finding was that each of these million-dollar projects failed because of "bad luck"— a fire, a flood, an earthquake, an influenza epidemic that put half the people on the project out of commission for weeks. We wrote a report on these findings and submitted it to a journal for review. Fortunately for us, one of the reviewers asked, "Where are your controls?" Duh!

We went back and found a dozen comparable projects that had succeeded. Lo and behold, each of these projects had also experienced "bad luck," but these projects had not failed because of it. When fire, flood, or earthquake destroyed their software configuration, they simply recovered their safe backups and returned to work. When half the team members were out sick, pair programming and technical reviews provided the redundant knowledge that allowed them to keep critical-path items moving along.

In other words, it wasn't bad luck but bad management that killed the first dozen projects. Realizing what doomed those projects gave me another way to identify badly managed projects: The project manager invariably invoked "bad luck" as the reason for failure.

Why do projects rush at the end?

I've never understood how someone can talk about "the nature of software" when software hasn't been around long enough for us to understand its nature. I've been around for almost the whole history of software, and I've participated in all kinds of software projects—embedded systems in cars, computer games, dating services, financial management, spaceship control, slot machines, pacemakers, digital watches, operating systems, smart cards, word processors, and many more. I've never found any commonalities—except that the quality of management seems to be the distinguishing factor between success and failure.

Good-quality management does produce a number of common patterns in software projects. [12] For example, when I see a software project that's not in a rush, let alone a panic, near the end, I know it has been a well-managed project. Sad to say, not many people have ever seen a well-managed software project and may not even believe such a happening is possible. "Software projects are always in a rush at the end," they say. "That's just the nature of software."

Though there may not be a "nature of software," there may be a nature of some badly managed software projects—with characteristics such as in the following sequence—that leads them to be in a rush at the end:

1. The managers don't understand the difference between testing, pinpointing, and debugging.

2. Because they don't understand the difference, they believe that testing caused most of the trouble in projects they've experienced.
3. Because they believe that testing causes trouble, they tend to postpone all forms of testing as long as they can.
4a. Because they've chosen their processes to postpone testing, testing is the first time they can no longer pretend things are going well.

Or, maybe, if the project is even more poorly managed . . .

4b. Because they've chosen their processes to postpone testing *and* they suffer from information immunity, they can pretend things are going well even after they've done some testing.
5. Because they suffer from information immunity, everything seems to be going "smoothly" through all the early stages of the project.
6. Because managers have stalled, bugs—many of which have lain dormant in the product since the earliest requirements—reveal themselves in late testing.
7. Because the entire system is now lumped together, many of these bugs are difficult to pinpoint, especially since developers cannot help pinpoint because they are now running around like headless chickens trying to cope with the sudden bug glut.
8. Because developers working under deadline pressure make new errors when trying to fix newly found errors, tempers flare, minds numb, absenteeism mounts, meetings proliferate, and strategy backfires.
9. And so the participants conclude, "We didn't have any problems until we started testing. We were right on schedule. Testing screwed up everything."

Burdened with that conclusion, managers begin planning the next project—the next panicky disaster.

To be sure, there are many other kinds of mistaken management responses—over-ambitious promises, under-provisioned tools, poorly staffed positions—all of which contribute to slow progress and lead to cutting test (and repair) time at the end. So, the first and foremost response to bugs should be to anticipate them. You aren't going to get lucky, so do the right things right from the start of a project. Prevent bugs by all means, then FFF the few that slip through.

How should you respond when close to the end?

But what if you haven't been doing the right things from the start? Unfortunately, once a project finds itself in the rush and panic of overwhelming bugs, there really aren't very many good responses left. If a monsoon of bugs turns up late in the project, all you can do is curse yourself for not testing early and often, and then moan, "Why do we never have enough time to do it right, but always have enough time to do it over?"

Even the best-managed projects will almost certainly have some bugs remaining as they near a ship date. Therefore, even in a well-managed project, the first response should be to schedule time for the endgame. Instead of a simple testing block in your plan, you need something that looks like this:

1. Stop all testing and start planning the endgame.
2. Rank the remaining known failures by significance.
3. Estimate how many of these failures, from the most significant to the least, your organization can reliably fix in the time remaining.
4a. Drop unfixable features from the shipment plan.
4b. Or if step 4a requires you to drop something that makes the product unacceptable, cancel and reschedule shipment.
5. Proceed to remove the bugs in order of significance as identified in step 2.

Why is this the proper response to bugs as the project ends? Well, when you reach the point at which you've decided to ship a product but you don't have time to fix any new bugs you detect, it makes sense to stop searching for bugs to fix. (If you have the resources, you may want to keep searching for bugs—not to fix now, but to report to customer support—but you'll need to resist the temptation to try fixing them in a hurry.)

Instead of trying to fix low-priority bugs, redistribute your fixing forces. In particular, clean up the significant bugs you know about, using your testers to help developers pinpoint the underlying faults. Then, manage tests to reveal any bugs in the fixes themselves.

Why are estimates of time that are needed for testing so far from reality?

Poor estimating at the beginning of a project is another reason we tend to rush at the end. It's not that the project is taking longer than it should, but that no one had the right idea of how long it should take in the real world.

The following subsections describe some common planning errors that lead to rushing at the end of projects as well as to sacrificed test quality.

Sunny-day estimating

There are several major reasons why estimating doesn't match the real world. One reason is so-called sunny-day estimating—estimating the time a project will take if everything goes as planned and there are no bugs to fix. What a dumb, dangerous concept! If there really weren't going to be any bugs, why schedule testing at all? Just write the code and ship it.

By using mathematical proofs of correctness, computer-science pioneer Harlan D. Mills and other writers thought they could build systems perfectly so that testing would not be necessary. They were moderately successful for some small, closed subroutines, but for several decades since, nobody has been able to write perfect programs for real applications. Moreover, the difficulty of doing so keeps growing as systems grow more complex. (We look more at this topic in Chapter 15.)

Unrealistic process models

Did you ever watch a house going up in your neighborhood and wonder why it took so long to complete the job once the house looked finished as you drove by? If you don't think clearly about house-building, you might assume that all that's involved is laying down a foundation, building walls, and putting on a roof. So, if you estimated how long it takes to build a house, but omitted the time it takes to do all the "invisible" finishing work, you didn't produce an accurate estimate. And if you believed your estimate was right in the first place, you would think it's taking an awfully long time to build the house.

Many estimates of software projects are wrong because they omit key steps. Commonly, they omit "finishing" steps such as pinpointing bugs, repairing them, then retesting and fixing the bugs generated in the repairs. Instead, the project estimate simply shows an undifferentiated lump of time at the end called "testing." This is akin to a house-building schedule that only includes "build foundation, put up walls, add roof, then finish up." "Finish up" glosses over at least half of the time needed to complete building a house—as it often does in software projects.

Poor-quality process data

Even when "finishing up" is broken more accurately into a series of test-pinpoint-repair-retest cycles, the estimate can be seriously wrong if it uses even slightly inaccurate input data. The following shows how one test manager came up with an eight-week, test-schedule estimate:

- I have 400 test cases.
- In previous projects, we found one bug for every five test cases.
- In this project, that would mean an estimate of 1/5 of 400, or 80 bugs.
- In previous projects, 2/5 of bugs were significant enough to demand fixing.
- In this project, that would mean an estimate of 2/5 of 80, or 32 bugs.
- In previous projects, about 1/2 of the remaining bugs needed to be fixed.
- For this project, that would mean 1/2 of 48, or 24 additional bugs, 56 total.

- Previous experience says we can find and fix about 20 bugs per week.
- That would mean about *three weeks* to handle 56 bugs . . .
- . . . BUT, 1/4 of those fixes will have bugs (14) and have to be cycled again,
- and that means *another week*, and will still leave 1/4 of those with new bugs (4).
- We should be able to clear up those 4 remaining bugs in *one week*, with one left.
- So, I'll add *one more week* for fixing.
- Then, add *another week* for triage to decide what's significant.
- And *another week* for testing to start up and build a backlog of bugs.

That makes a total of eight weeks, five after they actually start feeding bug reports to the developers to try to repair, not the three weeks that a less-aware manager might estimate.

This estimate assumes that the project will be properly staffed and coordinated. Myself, I would add 25 percent of the projected test schedule to allow time in the schedule for sickness, blocking problems in hardware and software, last-minute changes, and other such unplanned events, making ten weeks total for that lump called "testing."

These estimates are based on experiential data collected from past projects, but the relationship between past and current project estimates is not always simple. Suppose these estimates are wrong. Consider the fault-feedback-ratio (FFR)—the percentage of fixes that actually feed another bug into the system. The estimated FFR is 25 percent, with one new bug introduced in every four bugs fixed, but in my experience that's actually rather low. Many organizations I consult with would be delighted if their FFR were as low as 50 percent, with one new bug being introduced for every two fixes. Remember, fixing under pressure tends to raise the FFR.

Try re-estimating this test schedule with everything the same except change the FFR to 50 percent, introducing one new bug with every two fixes:

- . . . *three weeks* to handle 56 bugs . . .

- . . . BUT, 1/2 of those fixes will have bugs (28) and have to be cycled again,
- and that means *another two weeks,* and will still leave 14 new bugs.
- *Another week* will clear these up but will leave 7 new bugs.
- And *another week* will clear these up and leave 4 more.
- We should be able to clear up those 4 remaining bugs in *one week,* with one new bug left. Actually two, but maybe with enough people around having nothing else to do, we can reduce the FFR for that week.
- So, add *one more week* for fixing.
- Then, add *another week* along the way for triage.
- And *another week* for testing to start up and build a backlog of bugs.
- And then add 25 percent for unpredictable events.

The change of FFR from one out of four to one out of two stretches the "test" time from ten weeks to *fifteen weeks,* although the longer time means even more chance for something unpredictable to happen.

I have seen FFRs as high as four out of five. You might try to re-estimate this schedule using that FFR, or changing the fix rate. Remember, though, that if you try to speed up the fix rate, you're likely to raise the FFR.

No process data

Unfortunately, much estimating of testing is not based on data at all, but merely on a *wish* based on externals, with no adjustment of scope or process to trim down the wish to fit reality. Often, it goes like this:

"Oh, we absolutely need this software in place twenty-four weeks from tomorrow. We need two weeks to staff up and get approvals. Then we'll need four weeks for requirements, four weeks for architecture, four weeks for design, and eight weeks for coding. That adds up to twenty-two weeks, so we'll have two weeks left for testing."

When design slips a week, the managers have a big meeting and say, "Oh, we can still make the schedule. We'll just chop a week off testing. One week for testing should be plenty as there won't be many bugs—the developers are very, very good."

Determine whether you've passed the point where you can make a difference.

Perhaps the most important response to test information is making a decision about whether any response can improve the software itself. To do this, you may have to wait a while for more information. Waiting is an acceptable response, as long as you make clear why you're waiting. Never announce that you're "just waiting," but always refer to a specified event or time, or both.

Although seeking more information is an acceptable response, remember that your response is not simply your words. People listen to your tone and watch your body language. All parts of your response can affect morale, so keep your responses open, clear, and honest.

But what if you can wait no longer? What can you do if you have no time to get more information? Surprisingly, you still have many alternative responses. You can ship the product as is, you can feature the failures, you can warn customers about failures, you can withdraw parts, you can withdraw the whole product, or you can start over from the point at which things began to go wrong (a point in time distinctly different from the point at which *you noticed* that things had gone wrong).

The most drastic response would be to declare the project bankrupt and start over from scratch. This response may cost you your job, but save your life. Whether or not it costs you your job, you can begin the next project using all the learnings you've gleaned from this one. You've paid the tuition; the learnings are optional.

Summary

If a project hasn't been managed well before testing, most good responses will no longer be available. In many cases, there is no response that will save the project—except starting over and doing it right from the beginning.

Common Mistakes

1. *Depending on luck:* Luck favors the well-managed project.

2. *Reducing test time and resources to make a schedule:* If you don't care about quality, you can make any schedule, but then why test at all?

3. *Failing to adjust schedules and estimates as testing provides information on the actual state of the product:* Nobody knows the future well enough to make absolute promises. Anyone who can make promises about the future must be some sort of devil.

4. *Failing to collect process data:* Errors are made, not born. The more you know about where and when they are made, the easier they are to detect, pinpoint, locate, and fix—or prevent the next time around.

5. *Not understanding when testing starts:* Testing starts at project conception, or before. If you don't know this, you don't understand testing at all.

6. *Testing a dead horse:* If you see that a particular build is crippled and needs a lot of fixing work, don't blindly continue to test and report bugs, because the extensive fix will render your bug reports moot. [13]

15

Preventing Software Testing from Growing More Difficult

"If the fool would persist in his folly he would become wise."
—William Blake, Poet, Painter, and Engraver (1757–1827),
"Proverbs of Hell," *The Marriage of Heaven
and Hell* [1790–1793].

If you're going to do your next project better than you did the last, a good place to start is by understanding why it's actually going to be a more difficult project than the previous one. If your project was folly, all the more reason to persist—not in completing or validating that project, but in learning from that project.

Why is the situation growing worse?

Fundamentally, software testing is becoming more difficult because we have become more ambitious. We can see the infinite potential of computers, so whenever we succeed in creating software that provides something of value, we pause for a microsecond to say "thank you"—then demand MORE!

So, over time, systems grow larger. Fifty years ago, a program that used 87,000 bytes of memory would have been considered huge. Today, the word processor with which I wrote this passage uses 870,507,943 bytes, ten-thousand times as big as "huge" was then.

Offhand, a ten-thousandfold increase in size would seem to explain why testing has grown so difficult, but the story doesn't end there. Back in the late 1940s when World War II ended, the United States was abuzz with energy to restore normal peacetime activities—and ambitious engineers had an opportunity to do many things from scratch, and do them right. In the chemical processing industries, for example, many new plants moved from the drawing board to construction. One prevailing theme was the economy of scale—bigger would be better because bigger would be cheaper. The reality proved quite different.

Yes, having bigger plants reduced the unit cost of producing each gallon of a given chemical—but only when the plant was producing. When it was shut down, the cost was infinite. And why would a plant be shut down? Because of failure, of course— in software terms, a bug. As it turned out, in the bigger plants, the cost of failure was greater than the savings of scale. The passion for bigness died. Let's see why.

First of all, of course, the bigger the plant, the more places there were where failure could occur (number-of-failures). Is this true of software, too?

Second, the bigger the plant, the harder it was to pinpoint the cause of failure (time-to-pinpoint). Software, too?

Third, the bigger the plant, the harder it was to fix a fault without producing side effects (time-to-fix). Software, too?

Fourth, the bigger the plant, the greater the loss in productivity each time the plant shut down for repair (lost-opportunity-cost). Software?

As soon as the chemical companies began to realize how all these factors multiplied together to raise the cost of scale beyond the economies of scale, they abandoned construction of some of their largest plants and redirected their attention to building smaller plants. Can software makers learn from their costly lessons? What can managers do besides abandoning ill-understood projects?

Keep systems as small as possible.

The first counteraction to escalating testing costs is to keep systems as small as possible (but no smaller). Keeping requirements under control is largely a management job, outside of the development project itself. It is a management failure when this is not done well.

Uncontrolled growth of a system's requirements is so common that software analysts, designers, and developers have several names to describe the phenomenon: requirements leakage, requirements creep, requirements drift. It's just all too easy to agree to "add just one more thing" to a contemplated or ongoing project, especially if you don't have a process for estimating what nonlinear effects the addition will have on error cost.

Controlling the growth of requirements is made even more difficult because it requires that a decision-maker or stakeholder distinguish between something that really is *necessary* to the product versus something that would have value but whose value isn't worth the additional cost and risk. "Requirements discovery" happens when testing causes developers to realize "Hey—that really is a requirement!" Much of which we call *leakage* or *creep* or *drift* is recognition of some buried assumption, some requirement that was missed in the earlier requirements process.

One common mistake developers make is trying to handle every possible situation in the software. Just because you *can do anything* in software does not mean you *should do everything* in software, all in the same system.

I once had a client that calculated and paid mineral-rights royalties to landowners according to the terms of more than 15,000 leases, seven of which were exceedingly old and had a large number of "exception" conditions. When the client tried automating its manual royalties-payment system, its lease-specific software project was bogging down in testing. I was called in to help, and suggested that, for the time being at least, the client compute and pay royalties for these seven leases manually, as it had been doing prior to automating. This one change reduced the size of the system by half, and cut the development effort by a factor of ten. Not everything has to be done by computer, at least not all at the first go-round.

Keep your model of "system" expansive.

You might be successful in building a small application but run into trouble because the run-time or browser or operating system or network is big—and hairy. Further trouble may come from human beings who will interact with the application—they're the hairiest systems of all. Be vigilant in checking how the simple system you're developing is intertwined with larger, desperately complex systems.

Build incrementally in isolated components with clear interfaces.

The size of a program is not defined in terms of just the number of lines of code (forgive me for using that simplification earlier to make a point). Two programs of the same physical size can differ greatly in their internal complexity, which, in the end, can be a dominant factor in how difficult the testing effort will be. To help keep testing under control, you can take steps to control complexity. For instance, as suggested by the not-all-at-once strategy, you can build incrementally, with each piece built, tested, and fixed before the next piece is attempted.

There are a number of process disciplines that employ this incremental philosophy, many falling under the rubric "agile." The foundation of any such method is to build pieces small enough so that you have a high probability of leaving no bugs in the finished product. Why? Because to the extent that you're sure any new bug is not in your "completed" work, you vastly simplify the pin-pointing of bugs in the next component you add to the system.

Along with such incremental building goes the idea of test-first—creating a set of acceptance tests before you start to build each component. When the new component passes these tests, then you're ready to add it to the incrementally developing system, now to test it aggressively, in an investigative rather than confirmatory way.

There's another advantage to incremental development, as long as it is also guided by a significance-first process. If you run into something unexpected and have to stop before you planned to stop, you will at least have done the most significant things you could have done in the time you had. Thus, even if you run into unexpected problems (and you will), you can deliver something on schedule that's likely to be useful, even if not ultimately complete.

And sometimes, when the system is in use, you will discover that it's not worth adding those additional parts, thus keeping the system smaller than you initially thought possible.

Reduce the number of bugs going in.

Testing difficulty is not simply a matter of how many bugs you take out of a system, but also of when they go out. In general, the earlier you get rid of a bug, the less it costs you.

People frequently confuse the time a bug comes out with the time a bug was put in. A bug that's revealed in a test near the end of the development process might have been put in at any time earlier in the process. One of the unfortunate things about the word *bug* is the way it suggests that errors creep into the product in some mysterious way. But they don't creep in; they're put in. By people. At any time. And, since you want to remove bugs as early as possible, it's important to learn when your development process introduces them.

All this suggests that testing must be started early, and maintained throughout. One way to do this, as we've seen, is by building incrementally, testing first. [14] That's not the only way, but the other ways are invisible to those who believe that the only kind of testing is running code on a machine. In the next chapter, we see why that isn't true.

Summary

Although poorly organized and executed testing can certainly prolong the effort, there are intrinsic system dynamics that make testing and fixing take longer as products grow larger and more complex. If you understand these dynamics, there are ways they can be countered, up to a point.

Common Mistakes

1. *Underestimating the complexity of old, patched-up code:* I wrote this section in my old, wonderful house in New Mexico as a plumber worked in the next room trying to unplug my sink. I had thought his job was going to be straightforward and comparatively simple, but he spent more than two hours trying to figure out how to retrofit what is conceivably sixty-year-old plumbing before he could clear the pipes. Complexity in drainpipes and in old, patched-up code can be similarly perplexing.

2. *Not allowing these matters to be discussed, let alone measured:* Any time you hear someone say, "We can't talk about that," you need to stop whatever you're doing and talk about it. The same goes for "We can't measure that."

3. *Failing to adjust process data as current experience indicates:* I don't know of any software development or maintenance project that doesn't contain surprises. That's one reason why testing can't be planned to perfection in advance, and has to be exploratory.

4. *Using early returns as indicators of later results:* One thing you always know about initial cases: They're different from later cases, by definition.

5. *Thinking about testers as "the bad guys who prevent delivery":* Like any human beings, some testers are bad guys, but good or bad, they are simply providers of information. They don't make delivery decisions—if they do, then their managers are the bad guys.

6. *Testers thinking of themselves as "quality police":* Even if they were police, they are certainly not judges or juries or legislators.

16

Testing Without Machinery

"Ninety-nine percent of all failures come from people who have the habit of making excuses."
—George Washington Carver, Inventor and Botanist (1864–1943), see http://www.worldofquotes.com/topic/Failure/index.html for this and other observations about why things fail.

The number one testing tool is not the computer, but the human brain—the brain in conjunction with eyes, ears, and other sense organs. No amount of computing power can compensate for brainless testing, but lots of brainpower can compensate for a missing or unavailable computer. This principle guides James Bach's effort to replace the term "manual testing" with the more relevant "sapient testing."

On his blog, at http://www.satisfice.com/blog/archives/99, James makes his point vividly: "Manual testing conjures images of chain gang laborers, moving rocks. You immediately wonder why they don't just use a backhoe."

Testing by machine is never enough.

The simplest way to put lots of brainpower to work testing a system is the technical review. A technical review takes place when peers sit down together as a group to analyze and document the good and bad qualities of some technical product, such as code, design, a specification, or a user manual. In the case of code, rather than treating the product as a sealed (or "black") box, the reviewers are said to be performing "white box" or "transparent box," or, even better, "open box" testing. And, though nobody is banging

142

keys, testing it is. Technical reviewing is indeed a process of "gathering information about a product with the intent that the information could be used for some purpose."

One obvious advantage of technical reviews is the way they can be applied to project materials that cannot readily be tested by machine. How do you test a feasibility study on a computer? Well, of course requirements and design documents can be subjected to machine tests for consistency and grammar—and such tests can be valuable—but they are sorely limited compared with what can be accomplished by several human brains working over the materials.

The choice between machine testing and technical reviewing is not either-or. Technical reviewing is an especially powerful testing technique when *combined* with machine execution testing because the two approaches tend to detect different types of bugs. Whereas either method alone—applied to code and done well—may find 60 to 70 percent of bugs, when combined they often may find 90-plus percent.

Still, many developers seem reluctant to participate in technical reviews, for a variety of reasons. [15] Curiously, the reasons given for not wanting to review a product can provide the perceptive manager with one of the most powerful, and quickest, ways of testing that product.

Instant reviews

Over the years, the most common complaint I have heard about technical reviews is that they take too long. One reason organizations that lack experience with reviews think they take too long is that their people don't know when a review has been completed. In many cases, a review actually may be finished before these inexperienced reviewers even recognize that it has started. I call these types of reviews, which occur when someone gives a reason why a work product cannot or should not be reviewed, "instant reviews."

The "reasons" listed below all pertain to someone's attempt to block a review. They are bugs in the thought process of the producers, not in the product itself, and are themselves instant reviews.

- *"It would take too long to review the product."* When you hear someone give this objection as the reason for not performing a technical review, the one issue to raise is that the product is not a suitable size, and must be broken down somehow into reviewable (that is, understandable) pieces.

- *"But the product can't be broken down into reviewable pieces."* In this case, the issue is that it's one big incomprehensible lump, and the review recommendation is to start over and rebuild it into something reviewable. If it's too big to review, it's definitely going to be too big to test in other ways.

- *"Nobody but the author could understand the code."* This product must be rebuilt into a form that can be used and maintained—unless you're willing and able to send the author along with every copy you deliver, now and for the entire lifetime of the product.

- *"It's self-evident."* If it's truly self-evident, why object to a review, which should take a few seconds? In my experience, the claim of *self-evidence* is never true. Perhaps a self-evident product exists somewhere, but in half a century, I've never seen a piece of software or supporting material that fulfilled this ambitious claim.

- *"It's too small to bother with. What could possibly go wrong?"* Well, if it's that small, a review will tell you quickly and cheaply what could possibly go wrong. You might want to remember the number of times a one-line code change has cost some organization a billion dollars or so, or the times that such a change has actually killed someone. The shorter the work product, the more likely people are to say it's not worth bothering with—and then to not bother to do it carefully, or to consider its interaction with and dependency on other systems, which may be huge.

- *"It's too late to review it."* It may indeed be too late in the development process to change a product, but the issue here is that something's wrong with the development process itself. Just don't be surprised when you start taking your lumps for all the bugs.

- *"It's too early to review it."* It may indeed be too early, but if your schedule says something is supposed to be ready for review and it's not, then the issue is that you're now behind schedule.

- *"Yes, it's time to review it, but I'm still fixing bugs in it."* If a product is very buggy, it's probably a good idea to review it immediately, to help out the developer, who is in some kind of trouble. If the developer refuses help, then *that's* the issue. No developer is good enough to consistently do it alone—and do it right.

- *"We can't review it because we don't know what problem it's supposed to solve."* Then why the heck did you build it? The issue here is that some ancestor document or process is not finished, or not understood. Or perhaps there isn't a problem the product is supposed to solve, in which case the instant-review recommendation is, "Throw it out and stop wasting money."

- *"The problem statement we have doesn't really address the problem we're solving."* Well, fine, so the issue here is to get the appropriate problem statement before proceeding—unless you expect future users and maintainers to be mind-readers.

- *"We don't know what problem we're solving because we're defining the problem as we go along."* I hear this complaint from clients who claim to be using some agile development process. Unfortunately, they don't understand how an agile process works, and they're reviewing the wrong pieces. In an agile process, you review each definition piece, or "story" (that is, each definition of the problem

145

to be solved by the next software increment); design an acceptance test; review; and then test the work product derived by both the developers and testers from the definition. You proceed incrementally in this way until your customer says there are no more stories to implement.

- *"We would have to spend weeks preparing for a review."* If people need weeks to prepare, it means they haven't been producing the deliverables that need to be tested/reviewed. A basic tenet of any development process worth its salt says you should be producing these items, so if you haven't produced them, then you haven't performed the entire process—and so the product is, by definition, not finished. Would you accept your car from the repair shop if the mechanic said it was repaired, except for the repair steps he didn't bother to do? No, this review is over.

- *"We don't want anybody looking at what we're doing, because our people are oversensitive."* Either the wrong people are working on the product, or they're being mismanaged. Or perhaps they're planning to use the program to steal something from your organization. Or extort something from you because they're the only ones who know anything about a critical program.

- *"You can't review for performance, because we don't know what that will be until we build it, and then we'll optimize so it won't be a problem."* Sometimes this excuse turns out to be valid, but why depend on luck? This product needs a review that simply asks the question, "Does this look as if it will have a chance to perform properly?" And, if the answer to that review is affirmative, then the next review should ask the follow-up question: "Is this written in such a way that future optimizers can understand it?"

- *"We'll let you know as soon as we're ready."* Review is over. Instant-review result: Review was not complete because the product was not finished.

- *"We builders reviewed it already, internally, so another review would be a waste of time."* If the product has been done well, a second review won't take long, and will give you assurance that someone other than the builders can understand it. If the internal review wasn't done well, then it's unlikely that the product was done well either.

- *"We reviewed something just like this before."* Terrific! That means you'll be able to review this new one all the more expeditiously. You may also be able to compare results from the two reviews, which will provide additional information.

- *"You and your reviewers aren't fully qualified in this area. In fact, the only qualified people are on this project."* If there really are no qualified reviewers external to the project, I guarantee that this product will be a never-ending maintenance problem, and will be vulnerable to major security problems.

- *"There's really nothing new here; it's all reusable code."* Wonderful! In that case, the review will be short and sweet—*if* we have documented evidence of the state of each reusable piece and its interfaces.

- *"If you follow the instructions, nothing can possibly go wrong."* This warning usually means the builders don't know what will happen if a user doesn't follow instructions. Besides, anyone who believes this fantasy about any piece of software just doesn't understand software.

- *"We [tested] [tried] [demonstrated] it, and it works okay."* The issue here is the definition of "okay," one of the most ambiguous lullaby words in the English language—and many other languages, too. Once "okay" is defined, then it will be possible to determine whether the work product does what it's supposed to do. Would you like to bet what that answer will be?

147

- *"It works."* Two more of the most ambiguous words in the English language are "it" and "works." Usually, in my experience, this pronouncement means: "We haven't tried very hard to make the product fail, and we haven't been running it very long or under very diverse conditions. So far we haven't seen any failures, though we've been generous in our interpretations, and we haven't been looking too closely, either."

- *"There's no problem at all!"* Wonderful! In that case, there will be no problem reviewing it.

- *"We've never encountered a difficulty."* Good for you. Now we'll see if non-builders are going to be as lucky. What do you predict?

- *"We didn't know it was so bad it had to be reviewed."* Don't use reviews as punishment for work you might believe is bad. Reviewing a product should be a standard, universal process. It shouldn't imply anything about a product's quality, but rather only about the importance of the product being "good"—that is, doing what it's supposed to do. So, being asked to have your work reviewed signifies that your work is important. Anyone giving this excuse doesn't understand the role of reviews. Or is your organization actually using reviews as punishment?

- *"We didn't know we needed to review it."* Then you don't understand your development process. The fix for this is education and communication.

- *"We're not ready because we are a bit behind, but we're hoping to get lucky and catch up."* The complete review report to management can be succinct: "They're hoping to get lucky." Hopefully, your management knows that luck is not an issue in software development.

- *"We think we're not doing a very good job, and we don't want management to find out."* Of course, you'll never hear this stated explicitly, but it's what many instant reviews detect. Interestingly, reviews generally show that these work products are not as bad as the builders fear, though not as good as they hoped.

- *"We don't want to cooperate with those process nazis."* This sentiment is rarely going to be voiced, but it may be the deeper reason behind other excuses: feeling pushed around instead of respected. Sometimes a review is an exercise in class politics—and the busybody class wants to demonstrate its power. If people feel this way, perform a quick meta-review—a review of your review system. This involves reviewing the review system explicitly, looking for process bugs such as using reviews as punishment, co-opting technical reviews into personnel reviews (rather than reviews of a product), or perhaps badly led reviews.

Worst–first reviews establish bug severity.

Some of the same instant reviews can be used once you get inside the review room. In general, the quickest reviews are done by working on a "worst first" basis. So, you simply ask each reviewer to start with the worst problem he or she has found and work from there down to relatively minor problems. If, for example, a program is using a defective algorithm, there's no sense worrying about spelling errors in the interface.

Reviewing is a type of testing. The worst bugs from a tester's perspective are those that block testing. Testing experience tells you that the most problematic bugs for testing also will be the worst for reviewing. Certainly, the worst bug for testing is any bug that blocks you from testing all or part of the object under test. The same principle applies to testing by means of a review. If a reviewer says, "I cannot understand this code well enough to be sure it works," this is a blocking issue, and thus has highest significance.

If you're puzzled by what to do when faced with some variation on these blocking statements, translate the objection into testing terms. For example, "We can't *review* the product because the customer doesn't want to pay for it" becomes "We can't *test* the product because the customer doesn't want to pay for it." You'll know what to do, though your customer might not. In that case, it's someone's job to make the consequences clear.

The truth is not always convincing.

Instant reviews provide an enormous amount of important and early information in exchange for a tiny investment of time. But be warned: Instant reviews may convince you, but you still may have to work to convince others. Understandably, they won't believe someone else can learn so much in such a simple way about something into which they've put so much effort.

Sometimes, you'll have to go through the pain of a full review so builders can see how a review result occurred. Sometimes, you'll have to start testing and let early test results reveal problems that should have been detected in reviewing. Sometimes, you'll just have to bring the instant-review results to management and let it decide whether to waste time convening a formal review. Gradually, your organization will learn to perform instant reviews itself, and then you'll find new sweetness in your entire development process.

Testers make valuable reviewers.

Managers frequently tell me that there's no need for testers to participate in technical reviews, explaining their viewpoint thusly: "Because testers don't write code, they can't find bugs." My response is, "That's simply not true. You don't have to know any programming language to find logic bugs, major design flaws, poor human-machine interfaces, specification ambiguities, and many other difficulties."

Even if it were true that testers will not find bugs in the course of a review (and it isn't), they would still be able to learn from the experience. The greatest single benefit that reviews have to offer is learning, in any or all of the following ways:

1. By observing the patterns of flawed thinking that developers are likely to produce, testers learn to compose better tests.

2. By reviewing specs early, testers get a head start on the scope of their test plans.
3. By gaining familiarity with designs, testers accelerate the process of detecting bugs and then helping to pinpoint them.
4. By participating in reviews, testers learn how to be better reviewers of their own test cases, test plans, test drivers, and tools. And, as an added bonus, they can get up to speed on a project much faster than those testers who simply sit and wait for the developers to give them something to test.

Summary

There are many ways of testing without involving computers, but no way of testing that doesn't involve using brains. Test early and often; use all the brains you can muster.

Common Mistakes

1. *Not recognizing the value of technical reviews as a complementary form of testing:* Without a process that includes regular technical reviews, no project will rise above mediocrity, no matter how good its machine-testing process.
2. *Falling for one of the many arguments for skipping technical reviews (or any part of your process, for that matter):* Roughly nine out of ten of the troublesome, error-prone components in any system have bypassed or short-cut one or more process steps.
3. *Using technical reviews as punishment:* Cultivate a climate where each review is actually a rewarding experience for all participants.
4. *Skipping reviews to save time:* Errors are the number one cause of lost project time. Skipping reviews always makes the project take longer.
5. *Failing to review designs and code for testability:* At least half of your testing costs can be cut before anybody ever runs a test, if only your systems are designed with testability in mind.

6. *Failing to include testers as reviewers:* Testers contribute their unique point of view to the effectiveness of a review. Testers also need the education each review provides.

7. *Failing to recognize the value of learning:* Ultimately, learning is the most valuable part of reviews. Perhaps you do not factor in learning because it can't be easily quantified. But it can be, if you really want it to be. [16]

17

Testing Scams

"In moments of weakness it is difficult
to resist infantile suggestions. . . ."
—Bertrand Russell, Mathematician and Philosopher (1872–1970),
The Conquest of Happiness
(New York: Liveright Publishing Corporation, 1996).

It's one thing to fall into the trap of believing testing fallacies. It's another thing to fall prey to testing scams. In both cases, we believe something because we so very badly want it to be true. But in testing scams, we allow ourselves to be gulled by those who will benefit by tricking us. Here are some warning signs that you're in danger of falling prey to a testing scam.

We'll sell you a magic tool.

When I lived in Crested Butte, Colorado, I sometimes hiked across the mountains to Aspen. There were five hiking trails that I knew of, all of them former toll roads left over from the old gold-mining days when the only way to reach Aspen was through Crested Butte.

As I struggled to breathe going up 13,000-foot and higher passes, I often wondered why there were so many toll roads. By the time I'd hiked all five, I knew the answer: There were multiple toll roads because not one of them was very good. Each road's builder must have hoped to make a fortune by constructing the last word in toll roads, but it was not to be. Eventually, someone decided it was easier to get to Aspen from another direction, and the toll-road-building business was abandoned.

When hiking on the fifth of those abandoned roads, stopping at the pass to catch my breath, I wondered if I might have an explanation for the vast number of software testing tools. Not that none of them are any good, but that none of them quite meets the magical promises vendors hype to sell them.

Back in Crested Butte and eager to test my theory, I looked up specs for and reviews of a dozen or so of the best-selling testing tools. Tool A claimed to save 80 percent of testing costs; Tool B claimed a savings of 75 percent. Could that mean that if I used A and B together I would save 95 percent of my testing costs? Gee, then I could add Tool C, which promised to save 50 percent, and I'd be down to 2.5 percent of my original costs.

Not a fair conclusion to draw? I thought it was perfectly fair because the promotional claims for A, B, and C each touted a "unique approach" to testing. If that were so, their results should be independent—so my calculation would be correct, and there would be no need for books on software testing such as this one. Not much need for testers, either, or to allocate time for testing in the schedule. A project manager's dream.

Here's the secret about tools: Good tools amplify effectiveness. If your testing effectiveness is negative, adding tools will only amplify the negativity. Any other claim a tool vendor or manufacturer makes is, most likely, some kind of a scam. The sections that follow tell more of the story of scams and scamming.

Our demonstration is a scam.

Axel Bass, the DataSpew salesman, tugs on the jacket of his double-breasted suit, smoothing out the wrinkles, before striding into Laverne Weaver's office, hand outstretched. Her firm handshake and direct eye contact convince him that she's all business. He knows his software tool can't match the performance of his competitors', so he's come prepared with a convincing argument.

Laverne motions to him to take a seat, then settles herself into the high-backed, leather, swivel-chair centered perfectly behind her imposing teak-and-glass desk. "Well, Mr. Bass. I understand there's a DataSpew report writer you want to sell me."

"Please, call me Axel." Laverne nods but says nothing, so Axel continues. "Yes, we think you'll find our report writer is the best on the market. In fact, we're so sure you'll find its performance outstrips our closest competitor, we're willing to give you a week-long free trial of both machines—and we'll throw in a performance engineer for the week to help you set up benchmark tests to compare the two machines side by side so you can see for yourself." Axel beams his best confidence-winning smile and sits back in his chair to wait for her response.

Laverne jots a few notes on a pad on her desk before replying. "Alright. I'm willing to take you up on your offer."

They discuss a few more details, and close their meeting by setting dates for delivery of the two machines and for Phyllis, DataSpew's performance engineer, to come on site.

Phyllis arrives at the appointed time on Monday and sets up both machines, explaining as she works that she will write ten test reports against data in a sample bug database. By Thursday, Phyllis has developed and executed ten test cases. Miracle of miracles, the DataSpew report writer is significantly faster than its competitor's machine in all ten cases.

Will Laverne fall for this scam?

Laverne may think she has seen tests comparing the performance of one report writer against another, but Phyllis was not testing—she was demonstrating. Consciously or unconsciously, the outcome is rigged. If Laverne buys DataSpew on the basis of this so-called test, she will have fallen victim to a subspecies of The Demonstration Scam. This rendition is The Performance Benchmark Scam.

As we've seen in previous chapters, demonstrations are not tests. They might educate a customer, but they are not tests because they are designed specifically to prove a point and, above all, to avoid surprises.

I know this from personal experience because, years ago, part of my job was to design performance benchmark tests as a sales tactic. For any two systems—my employer's product and Brand X—I could always create a performance "test" that would "prove" that my system was superior. And, if I'd been in the employ of Brand X, I could have "proved" that its system was superior to all others.

Phyllis's ten reports were designed to showcase the strengths of the DataSpew report writer. Of course, if Phyllis hadn't been able to create ten reports that demonstrated the superiority of her company's product, that would be interesting new information. In a negative way, an attempted scam that fails is a test.

With all these testimonials, it must be good.

Often, a vendor doesn't even need to use a demonstration to scam you. Sales literature frequently contains pseudo-test results (for example, product comparisons, certifications, or endorsements) that appear to contain information, but which really only identify charlatans who took a fee or some payment in kind for the use of their names. Buy a bottle of water in Italy and you'll find endorsements of the product from all sorts of "doctors" who claim all sorts of wonderful results if you drink the contents. Buy shrink-wrapped software in . . . oh, you know what I mean.

If you want reliable tool or software testimonials, get them in person. If possible, visit referenced customers, watch how the product is used in their normal process, and talk to people who actually do use it. If a vendor doesn't want you to do this, be suspicious. I've known automation vendors to bar from sales-pitch presentations anyone and everyone with hands-on experience. Such vendors want to sell only to the big wallets, and will do anything they can to prevent people who are actually using the tool from airing their experiences—whether or not the product gets a passing grade or is slammed.

We can scam you with our pricing.

By selling only to the big wallets, for a big price, vendors also enlist the effect of cognitive dissonance that prevents customers from complaining about poor performance. Victims of The High Price Scam may keep complaints about the product to themselves because they fear they would look stupid for having spent so much money on a useless tool. Moreover, testers who are forced to use the tool despite its not doing the job keep quiet to protect the wisdom of their boss's decision.

Related to The High Price Scam is The Low Price Scam: discrediting competitive tools with disingenuousness, suggesting, "With a price so low, how could those tools be any good?" I heard one vendor claim that open-source (free) tools are dangerous because they have "no support." This is simply a lie—it's trivial to hire the authors of open-source tools to provide support. Moreover, when I looked deeper into this vendor's own tech support, I found it to be entirely inadequate—though overpriced.

Vendors who attempt to discredit any negative testimonial from actual users perpetuate another scam. One salesman told me, "Technical people are naturally finicky, like cats. You really can't believe nine-tenths of what they say." Perhaps that's true, but at least a cat tells the truth 10 percent of the time, unlike certain salesmen.

Our tool can read minds.

I was talking with a project manager about tool scams when he offered to show me an automated test tool he had just purchased for a sum much greater than my consulting fee (and which, therefore, must have been a good tool). We walked into this client's test lab where Sherry, one of his testers, was using the tool.

"Tell Jerry what you're doing," the manager asked.

"You bet," she said, so excited she nearly jumped out of her chair. "I just wrote an automated test that proves the search software works!"

"Show me," I said.

Sherry launched the test. It opened the search form, entered query criteria, and clicked the Search button. When the script completed, a window popped up saying that the test had passed.

"Hmm," I said. "How does it know the test passed?"

"It just knows. The tool is smart enough to know." Sherry gazed happily at the green Pass.

"May I try something?" I asked.

"Sure," said Sherry and the manager in unison.

"Okay, can you lend me a developer for a few minutes? Preferably the one who wrote this search function."

We went out among the cubicles and found Melanie, the developer. I huddled with her and asked her to write me a little program with the same interface as her search program, but one that never actually searches and always returns a zero, regardless of the search criteria.

While I distracted Sherry, Melanie inserted the dummy search routine in place of the original. Sherry was so enraptured describing the tool's wonders, she didn't even notice what Melanie had done. "Could you run that test again?" I asked.

"Sure!" Sherry ran the test again. This time, the system displayed an error message, NO RECORDS FOUND, but the tool still produced a window declaring that the test had passed.

"Hey!" Sherry exclaimed, turning to me in anger. "What did you do? You messed up my test!" Sherry failed to see that Melanie and I had just proved that despite the cheerful green Pass on the screen, the test tool didn't "just know" whether the test should have passed or failed.

The real problem here is that the tool doesn't know what the system's response is supposed to be. Sherry believed the tool would miraculously know whether or not the software was behaving correctly. She was so certain the tool knew best that she wasn't concerned by the Pass report on a test of a program that didn't do any searching at all. She assumed the tool knew exactly what records should be found.

This is The Omniscient Tool Scam. The tool operates with such authority that the user assumes that it is actually testing at the same level of detail as a human operator. Some tool vendors encourage this mentality. After all, their business is selling tools. They sell their tools on the premise that the tool will test the software with minimal human involvement. But beware: Tools are just tools. They still need humans, thinking humans, to operate them meaningfully.

Early in my career, I had the good fortune to learn just how far people could go in fooling themselves with The Omniscient Tool Scam. I was asked to review a budget increase of 25 million dollars (doubling the current budget). The product to be built was not just an automatic tester; it was an "automatic debugger." The concept was that you put program X into this wonderful tool and out came program X with all the bugs removed. Apparently, it read your mind about what you wanted.

Believe it or not, the executives of this large computer company bought the argument and doubled the budget. So I learned that people can believe anything, if it sounds good enough. Buyer beware (of your own wishes).

We promise that you don't have to do a thing.

Have you ever had an offer like the following from a testing service? "We'll handle all your testing. We'll even write the test scripts. You just give us the software you want tested and leave everything else to us. We can do unit testing, positive testing, negative testing, boundary testing, functional testing, performance testing, load testing, stress testing, acceptance testing, and even high-leverage use-case synergistic data testing."

How tempting is this? Hand over your software, and all your testing headaches go with it. You'll never have to worry about that pesky testing stuff again.

The people in the testing service may, in fact, be capable of doing a good job. However, just like internal testers, they need to know what information they're supposed to be gathering. Someone needs to think through the value the testing service offers, the information it can reasonably be expected to uncover, and then manage the contract to make sure the testing service is indeed providing the kind of information the project management team most needs.

A related scam is The Outsourcing Bait-and-Switch Scam in which the vendor uses senior testers to attract a client but, once the contract is signed, replaces those senior testers with cheap, inexperienced, junior testers—often at the senior-tester price.

If it's too good to be true, it probably isn't. The "You Don't Have to Do a Thing" Promise is always a scam.

We are secretly in cahoots.

Some managers dream of controlling software development from a distance, merely using numbers instead of personal observation to, at the least, verify those numbers. When managers adopt this stance, they open themselves to collusion scams in which two parties get together to game the system.

Bugfests, for example, are easy to game. Here's how it works: A developer and a tester secretly team up. The developer inserts bugs just before the bugfest. The partner then "finds" these bugs and receives a bounty for each, after which the partners split the loot. I know of one instance where the tester bought a new powerboat with the bounty money before the scam was detected, but it's quite likely that most bugfest scams are never reported.

Another fine collusion scam has a tester reporting bugs secretly to a developer. The developer then pinpoints, locates, and fixes the bugs, then tells the tester to submit a report—which is then cleared an hour later. The developer gets credit for being the fastest bug-clearer. The tester may not be rewarded directly, but the developer usually finds a way. The first time I saw this collusion scam, the developer and tester were husband and wife.

Here's how to avoid scams.

One way to recognize scams is that they always promise something for nothing. The Performance Benchmark Scam promises that a vendor will provide lots of testing work for free. The "You Don't Have to Do a Thing" Promise suggests that it's only a matter of money, which is one version of nothing. The Omniscient Tool Scam presumes that a tool can operate without knowing anything about what you intended in the first place.

The same rule of thumb applies to testing scams as to con artists and telephone solicitors: If it sounds too good to be true, it's probably not true. It may be tempting to believe the results from biased or meaningless tests. It may be preferable to swallow faked results than challenge their creator. But testing scams result in a decision process based on invalid information. And as hard as it may be to turn your back on something that looks like a good deal, it's even harder to clean up the aftermath of accepting the deal. The only "something" you'll get for your "nothing" is regrets.

Summary

Whenever you're desperate to clean up the bugs and ship a product, you're vulnerable to a variety of testing scams that promise quick, painless relief.

Common Mistakes

1. *Relying solely on numbers to manage a project:* Numbers can be useful, but only if they're validated by personal observation and set in context by a story about them.

2. *Accepting testimonials through a third party:* Don't count on any testimonial you can't validate by talking directly to the person giving it.

18

Oblivious Scams

"The optimist sees the rose and not its thorns; the pessimist stares at the thorns, oblivious to the rose."
—Kahlil Gibran, Writer, Poet, and Artist (1883–1931),
The Kahlil Gibran Reader: Inspirational Writings
(New York: Citadel, 2006), p. 45.

It's bad enough that there are lots of scammers and vultures ready to take advantage of your desperation over testing difficulties, but the most frequent scams are unintentional, oblivious, self-perpetrated scams. They usually arise from optimism when we unconsciously ignore thorny bits of information, the pain of which would force us to realize how bad a situation really is.

What happens when we delay documentation?

Perhaps the most common case of such scamming occurs when testers wait until the end of the week to record the details of the testing they've done—the bugs and test data. A tester may need to wait a few days for interpretations of testing to gel, but nobody can remember exactly the detailed data of a full week of key banging. (That's why I recommended using tracing logs and tools half a century ago, and still recommend them now that we have even better technology available.)

Ambiguous test reports are like quicksand.

Language is rich with expression, which means that it can be expensive. For one thing, the same sentence can carry many different meanings to many different people, and different interpretations of test reports can be costly. One example to which I personally was privy came when I was helping a client assess the significance of the bugs uncovered by its testing. One particular feature was so buggy that I felt it should be removed from the product and rebuilt. The project manager was under the gun to ship the feature and asked me, "How bad is it really?"

"There's no more than one chance in a hundred that your customers will accept this as it is," I said, putting it as strongly as I could, allowing that neither I nor anyone else can know the future.

I went away, and when I returned the next month, I found that the manager had decided to ship the product—only to incur the wrath of his customers when this feature bollixed up their databases. "Why did you ship it?" I asked.

"Well," he said, "you told me there was a chance the customers would accept it."

"I said there was no more than one chance in a hundred."

"Right. So I took that chance."

When your job is on the line and you're given a chance to misinterpret an ambiguous statement, guess which way you'll interpret it.

Falsified test reports impede improvement.

Test reports are often scammed for humane reasons. James Bach tells a story in *Lessons Learned in Software Testing* of testers helping out the developers by not reporting bugs. [17] If testers feel they don't need to report the bugs as they find them, well, that in and of itself is information about the project. Do they feel the need to protect the developers from a blaming management? If so, I guarantee you'll find all sorts of scams in this organization calculated to mislead management—to the total disruption of effective project planning.

Or perhaps these testers were simply trying to reduce the overhead burden of keeping records. In that case, there's something wrong with the record keeping, but the scam prevents management from knowing what needs fixing.

The reason this excuse works is that sometimes the reasons are truly humane. James shared with me what he learned in that situation: "I was part of management for that project. I was free to change the process if I thought it would solve an important problem.

"Agreeing to defer officially reporting bugs was indeed information about the project: I hope it is information about the flexibility of management to work with people in ways that are okay with them, as opposed to bringing my management hammer down on people's heads. I was trying to build some trust in that group. It was also information that we had a developer who was rather high strung.

"I agreed to postpone reporting officially, not to avoid it entirely. We made the process less bureaucratic, is all.

"By making that agreement, I was able to get earlier access to the code without using my management hammer.

"There's also an interesting postscript. About five years after that incident, I met that programmer [the high-strung developer] again, and reminded him of our arrangement. To my surprise, he said, 'Yeah, I was such a jerk back then. I should have just let you test the product, unconditionally.' People grow."

Indeed they do, and creating an environment for growth is always a good management approach. Just be careful you understand all of your true reasons for deviating from a successful process, and what accidental messages you might be sending.

Take your revenge somewhere else.

Sad to say, not all falsified test reports are trying to make developers look good. If relationships between testers and developers are strained, it's easy for testers to make particular developers look as if they're doing a poor job. Generally, this is an unconscious skewing of tests run and of the testers' assessment of bug significance, but it can be done consciously and maliciously. If so, it's a sign of a sick organization.

Early returns will mislead you.

Another common self-perpetrated scam is predicting how long testing will take based on early returns, as in the following proclamation: "Let's see, we fixed twenty bugs in the first week, and we have two-hundred known bugs, so it will take ten weeks overall to finish." No, not true. Generally speaking, the first twenty bugs you fix are among the easiest bugs to fix—they're the ones you fixed first, so (almost) by definition, they were the easiest ones to fix—so this "method" seriously underestimates how much time will be needed to fix the other 180.

The same type of error occurs during beta testing. Early users of a product are less likely to exercise the product in depth—and may, in fact, be blocked by bugs from even trying certain features. Thus, beta-testing results tend to seriously underestimate bugs in the less common features of a product. Rather than using some bogus "statistical" reasoning, you may want to analyze the kinds of problems that crop up in the doing of the testing itself (not problems in the product, unless the product is so hard to test that you can safely predict it will be an infinite process).

"Quantity" is not a synonym for quality.

Many oblivious scams depend on the fallacious belief that a large number either of tests run or of bugs detected necessarily means that a thorough job of testing has been done. If you fall for The Quantity-Means-Quality Scam, you expose yourself to all sorts of misleading information. Some common varieties follow.

The Thud Factor: One vice president of development was asked how testing could make his job easier. His answer surprised everyone: "I want thud factor in the test documentation. You see, our customers ask us, 'How do we know your stuff is any good?' all the time. I want to bring them a big, fat, test plan and slam it down on their desks to show them how important quality is to us."

In other words, if the thing you want to know about (quality) is too hard to measure, measure a substitute (in this case, thickness of documentation).

Hack-'n'-crack/Whack-a-bug: Bugs do not occur at random. If you fix each one as if it were an isolated case, you'll misestimate the amount of real accomplishment. Quite often, if you pinpoint the root cause of a failure, you'll explain—and eradicate—several failures at once. But if you treat each bug as an isolated, random event, you'll take a lot longer and miss quite a few bugs you could have easily removed. Or, you'll remove bugs you didn't know you were removing, and overestimate the amount of work remaining.

Regression Tests ≠ New Tests: If management rewards testers for performing a large number of tests, you may find that automated regression tests are counted each time they are run. Even if large numbers of tests were significant, counting the same test multiple times is a scam. If anything, the more times a regression test is run, the worse that augers for the product under test, and the process. Why run a regression test multiple times unless it takes you multiple times to fix the same problem?

Counting ≠ Thinking: Counting tests can produce many sinister effects. For instance, when tests are counted, testers may avoid creating any long or complicated tests. They may stop helping each other with tests, and stop doing other useful testing activities that don't count as test cases. Often, they find ways to copy tests with slight variations and call them different tests.

It's so tempting to substitute test counts for observation, conversation, and thinking. Reducing everything to bare numbers allows fabulous efficiency because of all the things we can just assume without having to hear them. And of course this creates a reservoir of lies by omission. It's so easy to lie by allowing your listener to continue making false assumptions about what you're doing.

Bugfests: We've already seen how bugfests can give a false sense of progress. Lots of monkeys banging lots of keys does not constitute an effective measure of testing efficacy, but is merely another way to scam managers into thinking a great deal has been accomplished. Besides, if you find a great many bugs, does that mean the testing is effective or the product is lousy?

Don't count non-tests as tests.

Amazing as it sounds, testers sometimes try to scam their managers by claiming that a non-test is the same as a test, as the following scams illustrate:

The Nothing's-Changed Scam: The classic example of claiming "no testing equals testing" is the statement, "We already tested that, and nothing's changed." This translates into ". . . nothing's changed (that I can think of)." And, of course, it's those changes you don't think of that cause most of the newly introduced bugs.

The It's-the-Same-Thing Scam: A slight variation on the same theme is the statement, "I already tested X, and it's the same as Y, so I don't need to test Y." I remember a very costly mistake when a tester claimed that loading a system from a CD was the same thing as loading it from a disk drive. Maybe it should have been, but it wasn't. That's why we test—to see whether what should be true actually is true. In this case, all the CDs shipped to customers had to be recalled because they wouldn't load correctly.

The Partial-Test-As-a-Complete-Test Scam: Yet another common self-perpetrated scam arises when the tester interprets a partial test as a complete test, saying, "Yes, I tested all the values in the table." (After all, the tester tested the first value, the second value, a value in the middle, and the last value. That amounts to the same thing, doesn't it?)

It's too tidy to be true.

Imagine a scene like the following: Carlos and Paul are looking over their latest test report. "It's an interesting read," Carlos says. "Look at these graphs. Tidy. Nice. Textbook-quality, even."

"Hmm." Carlos peers over Paul's shoulder at the graphs. "I see what you mean. Curious. Let's ask Teri where she got them."

They catch Teri about to leave her office for a meeting. Paul holds up the charts. "This will just take a minute. We were wondering how you created these graphs."

"With a spreadsheet." Teri's expression betrays her puzzlement at such a question.

"No. We mean, where did the data come from?" Carlos asks. "How did you measure the test effort? How did you make the bug-find-and-close curves so smooth?"

"Oh, that. Management insisted I turn in a test report, but we hadn't been gathering any of the data. I did my best to estimate what the numbers would have been if we'd kept track."

Fortunately, Carlos and Paul know better than to be suckered by data that are too neat, too tidy, too perfect. Real data are never that neat.

Garbage arranged in a spreadsheet is still garbage.

Unfortunately, Carlos and Paul's management fell for Teri's unintentional scam. It held up her test report as an example to all other test managers of the kind of report they should be producing. They also distributed Teri's spreadsheet as a template for all the other testers to use. They fell not just for The Tidiness Scam, but also for The Spreadsheet Scam: If it comes from a spreadsheet, it must be right.

A spreadsheet, like any other computer program, exhibits the garbage-in-garbage-out property. How could it be otherwise?

Summary

When we want so much for everything to go well, it's all too easy to inject our fantasies into our data.

Common Mistakes

1. *Using early reports of errors from a shipped product to estimate total errors shipped:* Early on, users haven't yet explored the full functionality of a product, and less-frequently-used features may be more likely to have bugs.

2. *Making bug reporting tedious or inconvenient:* Test reports will be distorted by anything that discourages immediate recording of found bugs.

3. *Creating a blaming environment that encourages falsified test reporting:* You should never punish people for the content of their messages, no matter how unpleasant the message may be for you. To learn more about blaming environments, see "Beyond Blaming: Congruence in Large Systems Development Projects." [18]

4. *Rewarding form over content:* It's nice if reports are neat, but first and foremost, reports should be timely and accurate.

5. *Rewarding quantity over quality:* If you reward busyness, you'll get lots of tests, but not much testing.

Epilogue

"What the American public wants in the theater is a
tragedy with a happy ending."
—William Dean Howells, American Author and Literary
Critic (1837–1920), as quoted in Edith Wharton, *A Backward*
Glance: An Autobiography (New York: Scribner, 1998).

If you're feeling discouraged by all the difficulties of software testing, I'd like to give you a happy ending. Is that possible?

A happy ending won't be possible if you're one of those people who will be happy with nothing short of perfection. There can be no perfection in this world, so for you there can be no happiness.

But if you're of a more realistic bent, then, yes, there are numerous happy endings. How so? Well, the story of software testing isn't really a tragedy. It's a story of our struggles to transcend our all-too-human frailties. If you look at the situation in software testing as a process, not a state, then of course there won't actually be an ending, but the process has a chance of being happy.

For the process to be happy, we may have to slow down our ambitions a bit to allow the art of software-building to catch up. We may have to improve our testing practices to bring our work up to the best we know. And we will definitely have to master those emotions that tend to overwhelm our knowledge and logic as we near the scheduled end of our projects.

But if we take up the challenge to do these difficult things, then the next half-century of software development will certainly continue the astonishing progress we've seen over the past half-century. You can count on it.

Endnotes

[1]   See G.M. Weinberg, *The Psychology of Computer Programming: Silver Anniversary Edition* (New York: Dorset House Publishing, 1998) for more on this topic. Master tester James Bach asserts that I have already written a book about testing, saying "More than one, of course—perhaps all of your books have been testing books. *An Introduction to General Systems Thinking* is all about how to penetrate the illusions that surround technology. It's about how to approach and manipulate and observe and think about systems. It is not seen as a testing book, mostly because you didn't call it a testing book, and because you didn't do much to show examples of software testing within it. That's important, I guess, but still, your career and body of work have been all about testing, among other things."

[2]   For more on my thinking on these issues, see *Quality Software Management: Vol. 2, First-Order Measurement* (New York: Dorset House Publishing, 1993).

[3]   For techniques on spotting and using *all* information, see the four volumes of *Quality Software Management* (New York: Dorset House Publishing, *Vol. 1*, 1992; *Vol. 2*, 1993; *Vol. 3*, 1994; and *Vol. 4*, 1997).

[4]   First published in 1975, *An Introduction to General Systems Thinking: Silver Anniversary Edition* (New York: Dorset House Publishing, 2001) explores aspects of nonlinear systems thinking.

[5]   See Tom F. Crum, *The Magic of Conflict* (New York: Touch-stone, Simon & Schuster, 1987). The concept of fantasy as reality is further developed in Gerald M. Weinberg, *More Secrets of Consulting* (New York: Dorset House Publishing, 2002), p. 34ff.

[6]   The idea of the full message going unspoken—and ways to discover the missing element—is further explored in Gerald M. Weinberg, *More Secrets of Consulting* (New York: Dorset House Publishing, 2002), p. 130ff. See also G.M. Weinberg, *The Secrets of Consulting* (New York: Dorset House Publishing, 1985), p. 84.

[7]   Developers and programmers seem to take pride in their ability to make features of their failures. For examples taken from all walks of life, see Gerald M. Weinberg, *The Secrets of Consulting* (New York: Dorset House Publishing, 1985), pp. 43–45.

[8]   The subject of expectations is so important that rather than try to treat it within the context of this book, I refer you to what many consider to be the definitive work. See Naomi Karten, *Managing Expectations* (New York: Dorset House Publishing, 1994).

[9]   Every person sooner or later must learn the value of this lesson: "Put your money where your mouth is." For more on the topic, see Gerald M. Weinberg, *The Secrets of Consulting* (New York: Dorset House Publishing, 1985), pp. 135–36.

[10] See William E. Perry and Randall W. Rice, *Surviving the Top Ten Challenges of Software Testing: A People-Oriented Approach* (New York: Dorset House Publishing, 1997).

[11] Even simple words can get in the way of effective communication. For more on this topic, see http://www.ayecon ference.com/Articles/LullabyLanguage.html. See also G.M. Weinberg, *More Secrets of Consulting* (New York: Dorset House Publishing, 2002), p. 27ff.

[12] The topic of patterns in software projects has long absorbed the IT industry. For a comprehensive treatment, see Gerald M. Weinberg, *Quality Software Management, Vols. 1–4* (New York: Dorset House Publishing, 1992–97). For a compelling look at how pattern recognition can be key to steering a project toward failure or success, see Tom DeMarco et al., *Adrenaline Junkies and Template Zombies* (New York: Dorset House Publishing, 2008).

[13] War stories keenly illustrate this point in Cem Kaner, James Bach, and Bret Pettichord, *Lessons Learned in Software Testing: A Context-Driven Approach* (New York: John Wiley & Sons, 2001).

[14] James Bach, after reading this material in my manuscript draft sometime during the summer of 2007, asked me whether I remember long ago asserting, *"The lesson of considering testing when coding should not be forgotten. Probably no single testing technique is of more value than foresight."* These words appear on page 377 of *Computer Programming Fundamentals*, 2nd ed. (New York: McGraw-Hill, 1966), a book I wrote with coauthor Herb Leeds. James was just discovering the book: "I have this open in front of me because it was cited in [William] Hetzel's 1973 book, *Program Test Methods*, as an exception to the rule that programming books provided only dismal testing advice. Your book was published the year I was born. I'm only now getting around to reading it."

Well, my memory isn't that good, so I don't remember those exact words, but at least I haven't forgotten the principle. We did know a few important things back then, but each generation has to discover them for itself.

[15] For comprehensive details both on getting stakeholders and on running technical reviews, see Daniel P. Freedman and Gerald M. Weinberg, *Handbook of Walkthroughs, Inspections, and Technical Reviews*, 3rd ed. (New York: Dorset House Publishing, 1990).

[16] To learn about quantifying the "unquantifiable," see *Quality Software Management: Vol. 2, First-Order Measurement* (New York: Dorset House Publishing, 1993).

[17] For the full story and others that will get your blood circulating, see Cem Kaner, James Bach, and Bret Pettichord, *Lessons Learned in Software Testing: A Context-Driven Approach* (New York: John Wiley & Sons, 2001).

[18] For this article, which I coauthored with family therapist and Satir Institute principal Jean McLendon, see "Beyond Blaming: Congruence in Large Systems Development Projects," *IEEE Software*, Vol. 13, No. 4 (1996), pp. 33–42. The article is also available online at http://www.ayeconfer ence.com/Articles/BeyondBlaming.html.

Additional Reading

For those who wish to continue with their exploration of the world of software testing, I recommend all of the following.

Beizer, Boris. *Software Testing Techniques*, 2nd ed. New York: Van Nostrand Reinhold, 1990.

> *A textbook for software testers, covering pretty much all the technical issues as of the date of publication.* With Lessons Learned in Software Testing, *it covers both ends of the conventional-radical software-testing wisdom.*

Copeland, Lee. *A Practitioner's Guide to Software Test Design.* Boston: Artech House, 2004.

> *This is an excellent reference or textbook providing a solid overview of the most common test methods.*

Kaner, Cem, James Bach, and Bret Pettichord. *Lessons Learned in Software Testing: A Context-Driven Approach.* New York: John Wiley & Sons, 2002.

> *Lots of accumulated wisdom for testers and managers, from three leading lights among testers. It is not a textbook, and not to be read at one sitting, but keep it on your desk and pick it up at least once a day, and open at random to learn a useful tip that will improve your job performance.*

Perry, William E., and Randall W. Rice. *Surviving the Top Ten Challenges of Software Testing: A People-Oriented Approach.* New York: Dorset House Publishing, 1997.

> *Short, sweet, and to the point, this book highlights many of the most important human issues in software testing.*

Index